T0116870

Conversations with God

KENNETH A. BROWN

WESTBOW
PRESS

A DIVISION OF THOMAS NELSON

WestBow Press books may be ordered through booksellers or by contacting:

WestBow Press
A Division of Thomas Nelson
1663 Liberty Drive
Bloomington, IN 47403
www.westbowpress.com
1-(866) 928-1240

Because of the dynamic nature of the Internet, any web addresses or links contained in this book may have changed since publication and may no longer be valid. The views expressed in this work are solely those of the author and do not necessarily reflect the views of the publisher, and the publisher hereby disclaims any responsibility for them.

Any people depicted in stock imagery provided by Thinkstock are models, and such images are being used for illustrative purposes only.

Certain stock imagery © Thinkstock.

ISBN: 978-1-4497-2710-9 (sc)
ISBN: 978-1-4497-2711-6 (hc)
ISBN: 978-1-4497-2709-3 (e)

Library of Congress Control Number: 2011917016

Printed in the United States of America

WestBow Press rev. date: 10/5/2011

Dedication

This book is dedicated to the six congregations among whom I have been privileged to serve.

Tottenham Baptist Church, London, England
West Leigh Baptist Church, Leigh-on-Sea, England
Cameron Memorial Baptist Church, Regina, SK, Canada
Heritage Park Alliance Church, Windsor, ON. Canada
Community Congregational Church, Lathrup, MI. USA
Bloomfield Hills Baptist Church, MI. USA

In addition, there are all those who have assisted me and inspired me as I prepared this book: -

My wife Elaine, for her encouragement and patience in making corrections to the manuscript; to our son Cameron for his design of the cover; to Tom Cobb for pressing me really hard to publish my prayers and for all the assistance he has given me to bring this project to completion; and to the staff at WestBow Press who have spent much time in assisting and encouraging me.

"Any man who will look into his heart
and honestly write what he sees there
will find plenty of readers."
Edgar W. Howe

Foreword

"The prayer of a righteous man is powerful and effective."
James 5:16 (NIV)

I had been away from my home church for several weeks and upon my return, noticed a man whom I did not recognize. Since he was seated near the pulpit, I assumed he was going to have a speaking part in the day's activities. I was, of course, curious as to who he was and what he would speak about. He did in fact speak and I was immediately struck by his rich and very proper voice and speaking style, so much so that I have to confess I did not at first really pay attention to what he was saying. When the content and spirit behind that first prayer that I heard Ken utter reached me, I knew I had listened to something very different and uplifting authored by a unique man.

Although we seldom realize it at the time, we know that God's timing is always perfect. Ken's prayers were for me a perfect example. I had been struggling with a prolonged spiritual drought illustrated by my "production line" prayers each morning that were uninspired, unspiritual, and unfulfilling. I was experiencing, as Oswald Chambers put it, "spiritual leakage". As Ken said in one of my favourite prayers, I was "going through the motions of faith". Ken's prayers reminded me that praise must be the centerpiece of our devotions. That fact helped revitalize my faith. The great eloquence of his prayers lies in the fact that they are exceedingly well written and inspired by the Holy Spirit but at the same time user-friendly. You don't need a theology degree to benefit from them. He has a unique way of covering a wide variety of prayer-worthy subjects with the same smooth spirituality.

As blessed as I have been by his prayers, it has been even more rewarding to know Ken as a friend. I will always fondly remember our conversations that went far into the night when he was a houseguest. There may be a few worldly problems that we did not solve, but not many! Even my dog seemed fascinated by him! His warmth, wisdom, and grace taught me many things about my faith and I am eternally grateful for his friendship.

I wholeheartedly add myself to the long list of people who have encouraged the publishing of this book. All of us who have experienced periods of drought in our faith-walk need the refreshment that "Conversations with God" deliver so beautifully. Whether you are a pastor, leader or an individual yearning to serve and glorify God, this book will be a blessing to you.

Tom H. Cobb   **Bloomfield Hills, MI.**

Contents

A Word of Introduction . . .

Over the course of years many people have encouraged me to put my prayers into print. For various reasons I have ignored the idea. At West Leigh Baptist Church in England where I was pastor for 14 years I published one prayer a month in the church magazine for a while. Although this reduced the pressure on me to publish my prayers in a broader sense, it did not stop people asking me to publish. Wherever I have been involved in pastoral ministry, Cameron Memorial Baptist Church, Regina, SK., Heritage Park Alliance Church, Windsor, ON., Community Congregational Church, Lathrup Village, MI., Northwood Baptist Church, Royal Oak, MI., and more recently Bloomfield Hills Baptist Church, MI., the request to publish has always been present. I have never considered that my pulpit prayers were special in any way. But comments were made, such as, "when you lead us in prayer, it sounds as though you are talking directly to God". When you pray, "it sounds as though you expect God to answer". It was these kinds of comments that led me to explore more fully this whole realm of pulpit prayer. I assumed that every minister thought that he or she was talking to God when they led the congregation in prayer. It appears that the congregation didn't always feel the same way. Some felt that prayer was often misused to preach at the congregation. Others felt this was a time when it was hard to stay awake, particularly when one's eyes were closed! Some felt that the language and style was archaic and therefore it was difficult to follow along. There were those who felt it was very repetitive, the same things were said every week, particularly in churches that don't use a formal liturgy. The overall impression given was that this was a meaningless activity for many people and could be omitted from the worship service. Maybe there are some pastors who have come to this same conclusion and as a consequence have almost squeezed prayer out of the order of service. The result has been a poorer quality of worship. If we remove any direct interaction with God then all we are left with is ritual and rhetoric. None of these can lift the human spirit or transform broken and sinful lives. Only a direct encounter with God can bring about such changes in the citadel of the human spirit. I believe pulpit prayer is the doorway to such an encounter. We remove it at our peril. There are two main expressions of pulpit prayer:

- There is that which is set down in "a liturgy" that is repeated week after week.

- There is that which is frequently called "spontaneous" prayer. Here the minister or leader says whatever comes into his mind in any given moment as he feels inspired by the Spirit.

I would hasten to say that neither form is right or wrong. Both have their positive and negative sides. Saying the same thing over and over again means that often people no longer hear what is being said. Sometimes it doesn't reflect the way a worshipper is thinking or feeling at that particular time. On the other hand "all spontaneity" can get stuck in a rut to the extent that the worship leader is saying the same things week after week without realizing he or she is being repetitive. The only difference between the two is that one is read and the other is repeated with eyes closed. We need to remember that if David had not written down his prayers, there would be very little in the book of Psalms.

Public prayer has become one of the most difficult areas of worship. Hymns and songs can be chosen. Scripture readings can be selected to fit the sermon. The sermon can be prepared before time. But what about those times of public prayer?

The primary focus of pulpit prayer is conversation with God. If the worshipper should open their eyes, they ought to be looking to see to whom the worship leader is speaking. Prayer is always directed towards God and not the congregation. Prayer is not the time to score a few theological points over the congregation. When this happens it builds barriers to worship. This is an appointment with Almighty God. If you have an appointment with someone you usually prepare yourself beforehand. The same should be true for the worship leader, as much as for the worshipping community, as they approach that appointment with God. There are three areas that require vital preparation:

Personal preparation:
If the worship leader is not on speaking terms with God in his or her own personal life, it becomes very difficult to speak with God in public worship. A personal devotional life needs to be developed and nurtured. Time needs to be taken every day to talk to and listen to God. Pulpit prayer is but a reflection of personal prayer and the relationship we have with God.

Knowledge of the congregation:
If the worship leader is going to lead the worshipping community in prayer to God, it is important to know something of what the congregation is thinking and experiencing in their lives. It is important to reflect some of this in pulpit prayer. Pulpit prayer cannot be abstract. It has to be earthed in the experience of the worshippers and in the Word of God. When the worship leader is out of touch with the worshipping community, his or her prayers will not reflect their hopes and aspirations, their fears and defeats and their thanks and praise. It is these things that make prayer relevant and real in the worship service.

Preparation of your prayers:

Initially it is good to write out your prayers *the way you speak*. This way you can carefully prepare what you want to say. In this way you can bring people to the Throne of Grace where they can find grace to help in time of need. Prayers can be written out in full or they can be in note form. But preparation is vital! It is the only way to sustain a long pulpit ministry and stay fresh. That has been my experience. It is also alright to spontaneously add to the written prayer.

A word of caution:

There is always the danger of prayer becoming a presentation to God of a "wants list". Prayer must always be rooted in worship and praise. Even a quick glance at the Psalms in the Old Testament reveals that in most of the psalms they either begin or end with praise and worship. It is praise and worship that lifts prayer from being a "wants list", to a real encounter with God. It transforms prayer from being an intellectual exercise, to a time where we interact with God. It is in such moments that God can convict and reveal His will to His people. (See Acts 13:2-3).

The use of silence:

Sometimes worship leaders say too much. It can be very helpful during the prayer to allow time for silent prayer and reflection. This is often the time that the Holy Spirit will use to minister to people's hearts. So often we allow the clock to dictate the length of time that we spend in prayer and waiting on God. In Psalm 46:10 we read, "Be silent and know that I am God". (New Living Translation). Silence is a door of opportunity for God to interact with His people. Often silence is omitted because it allows us to look inwards and often we don't like what we see, so we omit those moments of silence. How often when we come home we turn on the radio or TV even if we are not listening or watching because the background noise stops us from thinking.

How to use this book:

If it is for *personal use*, then read the prayer through and make it your own. Let the first person plural become the first person singular. It might spark new thoughts and concerns for prayer and meditation. These can be written in pencil under the heading of "Personal Prayer Topics" or in a journal.

If you are using this book for *public prayer* at a meeting or in a worship service, it is suggested that you write out the prayer and adapt it to suit what is on your heart. In the sections where there is intercession, it will be necessary to suit the suggestions to the needs of the moment, both in your organization and in any situation requiring you to pray.

The purpose of this book is to encourage you to view prayer not as something that is only for the experts, but that it is an actual conversation between you and God. You may feel that it is important to keep a written record of your prayers so that you can see when God's answers come. This can form a basis for praise and thanksgiving and it will bring encouragement to the congregation.

It is my prayer that as you read through the pages of this book, that they may stimulate a greater desire to pray. In addition, those whom you lead in prayer may be encouraged to exercise a fuller ministry of prayer. May God enrich your prayer life and the life of others as you meditate on the ideas that you find on these pages.

> "We must move from asking God to take
> care of the things that are breaking our
> hearts, to praying about the things
> that are breaking His heart."
> *(Margaret Gibb)*
> †

1.

OUR GRACIOUS GOD AND Father, we express our praise to you this morning. Even in this dark and evil world, where man's inhumanity to man tears us apart and causes us much inward pain, we celebrate your majesty and power. You are the Sovereign God. You are on the throne of the universe. Nothing is outside of your gracious power and control. Father, you are here among us this morning. You are here to lead us to yourself and to reveal your heart and mind to us. You are here to deal with our sins and failures and to extend to us your forgiveness and reconciliation. You are here to minister to our hurts and pain. Lord, we magnify your name this morning.

Father, we must confess that we are often disturbed and discouraged to see the apparent success of those who oppose you and the work of your Kingdom - while your people wrestle with doubts, conflicts and difficulties of various kinds. Help us to accept the truth expressed by the Psalmist who said, "Do not fret because of evil men or be envious of those who do wrong." Father, we pray that you will minister your love and grace to our lives, that we may be strengthened; that we may see beyond the visible in order to see things as they really are. Lord, forgive us when we get bent all out of shape as we view the apparent triumph of godlessness.

Grant us courage O Lord, to put our lives on the line as we seek to communicate your truth to those around us. Where there is injustice, may we be able to diagnose its cause and declare its cure. Where there is bigotry, teach us how to love and how to encourage others to love. Where there is poverty, help us to share the wealth that we have received from your hand. Where there is tension and violence help us to be peacemakers that lead people to you, who are the Prince of Peace. Heavenly Father, help us to become what you have destined and empowered us to become. Where there is darkness, may we be your light to dispel the gloom. Where lives are dry and thirsty, may we be like summer showers that bring life and fruitfulness. Where there is ugliness and distortion enable us O Lord to portray the beauty of Jesus and the splendour of your will and purposes.

Let us have a time for silent prayer and reflection:

As we bow in your presence - our needs are known to you. Minister to us by the power of your Holy Spirit and as we fellowship with you, and with one another this morning, transform us we pray. Give to us a vision for the lost world around us. Empower us for ministry to others.

We pray for that troubled land of _____ and your people there, that the power and love of your Kingdom may be demonstrated in their lives. We remember all the Christian leaders there that they may have courage and wisdom to know how to assist your people.

We pray for _____ (a country needing relief) – and the Christian agencies that are seeking to help and that their ministry will be seen as a demonstration of God's love and concern ministered through His church.

Many of the problems facing us today have been caused through poor stewardship of the resources that you have provided for us. Forgive us for our greed and for viewing everything only from an economic point of view. O Lord, put a new spirit in the hearts and minds of people.

Lord, as we focus on your Word this morning - feed our hearts and minds, so that we may grow in grace and in our knowledge of you. Equip us, so that we may be able to minister to others; and Father, if our hearts are dry, if our lives are lived outside of Christ this morning, then Lord, enable us to reach out by faith and take hold of you, so that we may be spiritually renewed and restored to fellowship with you. These things we ask through Jesus Christ our Lord. **AMEN.**

Scriptures for personal meditation and reflection:

Job 36:22-23 : Romans 8:28-39 : Hebrews 11:3 : Mark 4:40-41

Personal Prayer Topics:

_____

_____

_____

_____

_____

_____

2.

FATHER, AS WE COME before you this morning, we lift our hearts to you in worship. You are a great and wonderful God. We are amazed that you have patience with us and desire to be the mainspring of our lives. We are so unworthy of your attention. We are so fickle in our allegiance. We are so sinful in our thoughts and deeds. Lord God, as we come into your holy presence this morning, cleanse us we pray from those things in our lives that distort your image in us. Help us to take down the barriers of sin that we so readily erect. Lead us Lord to the place where we can receive your forgiveness; where we can have fellowship with you and one another and be strengthened in our innermost being.

Father, when we focus our faith on you, we discover a new security to living. We discover that we don't need to live in fear. Even though our lives may not remain untouched by the storms of life and we may get wounded by the onslaughts of evil, we know, O Lord, that you don't leave us to suffer these things alone. You care for us in the midst of our conflicts. You bear the burdens with us as we share them with you. Lord Jesus, you understand us because you were despised and rejected by men, a man of sorrows and familiar with suffering.

We thank you, Father, for being by our side and raising us up to our feet every time we are knocked down. Thank you for leading us to victory. We so appreciate the fact that you feel our pain and that you bear our hurts, so that you can minister your grace to us and transform that which is ugly into that which enriches and blesses our lives and the lives of others.

Father, the world around us is a rough and hard place. Help us not to duplicate its spirit or its ways in our lives. May we be able to grasp more firmly your holy purpose for our lives. When our strength is spent, help us to draw upon your omnipotence. When we can't think anymore, flood our minds with your knowledge and wisdom. When we feel inadequate, help us to put ourselves in your capable hands. When there seems to be no way forward, help us to put our faith and trust in you.

Today, O Lord, we would pray for . . . .

- Those who bear the responsibility of government, both national and local, that they may not be governed by party policies but by your purposes.

- Those who serve you overseas as missionaries. They are your ambassadors. May they . . . . *(Name any that your group knows and add what you feel is their need . . .)*

- Your Church in places where there is conflict and strife. We remember in particular . . . . *(Research current news media)*

Gracious God, minister to us from your Word this morning. You know what we need to hear. Focus our attention on yourself and may we hear your Spirit speaking to our hearts as convictions are born and actions are contemplated. Minister to us, not according to what we want, but according to what we need, so that every fibre of our being and every activity of our lives may declare your praise and glory. This we ask through Jesus Christ our Lord. **AMEN.**

Scriptures for personal meditation and reflection:

Psalm 51:1-19 : James 5:13-20 : 1 John 1:1-10 and 2:1-17

Personal Prayer Topics:

_____

_____

_____

_____

_____

_____

_____

_____

3.

FATHER, AS WE COME into your presence this morning, we do so with praise on our lips and a desire in our hearts to know you better. We bow before your majesty. As we move into your presence, we find ourselves strangely quiet. The thoughts that buzzed through our minds earlier become strangely silent. As we see your glory and power revealed in your Son, the Lord Jesus Christ, and declared in your Word and manifested in the lives of our fellow believers, all we can do is to bow before you and quietly and reverently worship you in awe and wonder.

Let us have a time for silent personal prayer and reflection:

As we look at your strength and power, we see our own weakness and ineffectiveness. As we see your love, we recognize the poverty of our own. As we look at your holiness, we realize our own sinfulness. Lord God, minister to us today. Grant us your grace of forgiveness. Cleanse us from every stain of sin. Break the power of Satan's hold over our lives, we pray.

Lord God, there are times when we come to worship and we don't feel like worshipping. We feel distant from you. We feel battle weary on account of the circumstances of our lives. Sometimes, O Lord, we come wondering where you are, as we feel so alone and so empty, and so fragile. Father, let the wind of your Spirit blow through our lives this morning, sweeping away those things that would hold us down and stop us being what you want us to be. O God our Father, restore us and renew us we pray as we draw near to you this morning. May our lives be open to you. May your purpose be fulfilled for our being here today.

We pray for those areas where there is armed conflict and nationalism has become a destructive force of evil. Lord God, put a new spirit into the hearts and minds of people, that peace and a sense of community might be restored.

We pray for those who have obeyed your call to serve you overseas. Equip them we pray for the challenges they face every day. Give to them wisdom and strength of purpose. When despair begins to overwhelm them, bring to them new hope. May they see lives changed and people brought to a saving knowledge of Jesus Christ through their ministry. May your hand of protection overshadow them.

So Lord, as we look again at your Word this morning, grant that your Spirit may be able to speak to our hearts and minds. May your Word help us to see your will for our lives. May it nourish our innermost being – and by so doing, equip us for the challenges that face us during this coming week. These things we ask through Jesus Christ our Lord. **AMEN.**

Scriptures for personal meditation and reflection:

Psalm 27:1-14 : Psalm 34:1-22 : Psalm 140:1-13

Personal Prayer Topics:

_____

_____

_____

_____

_____

_____

_____

4.

*L*ORD, AS WE COME into your presence today, it is because we want to get to know you better. We want to bring joy to your heart as we walk in your ways and carry out your purposes in our lives. Father, we desire this morning more than anything else that we might be at the centre of your will and that we might live within your design for our lives.

Lord, you have fashioned us with your hands and created us for your glorious purposes. You have stamped your image upon our hearts. Therefore this morning, O Lord, we recognise that our deepest longings can only be fulfilled in you.

Let us have a short time for private prayer and reflection:

As we continue in your presence we also recognise that our instincts are so earthbound. The delights of this life tantalize and tempt us. It seems O Lord, that there are innumerable enemies deep within our souls that thwart our attempts to please you. Father, we fail so often to do what we really want to do. We fail to grasp what we are reaching for. So often we fall back in shame and feel flattened by despair. Lord, forgive us this morning. Restore us we pray. Make us whole through the life giving power of the Lord Jesus Christ.

Lord, you have shown us how much you love us. You have declared your ways to us through your Word. Help us by the power of your Spirit to translate your truth into our daily lives. Father, we praise you because you love us even when we fail to respond to you in loving obedience. When we cannot understand you, you understand us and continue to hold on to us. Lord, when we fall short of our sincere intentions to abide within your will, you rekindle the fire within us and empower us to do that which we know we cannot do by ourselves. Grant us your grace this morning to walk in your ways and to have the joy of knowing that we are pleasing you. Heal our brokenness. Remove the causes of our pain. Encourage us with your love. Plant seeds of positive hope within our hearts. As we release our burdens to you, may we grasp more firmly the grace you give to us.

Father, we pray this morning for . . . . (Expand these topics)

- The city of _____ with its . . . .
  (Naming specific needs . . . .)
- World leaders as they struggle with vast economic problems
- The Church - as it cares for people; proclaims your Word; demonstrates your power

Lord, as we bow before you, we know you understand us! Please minister to us according to our needs. Where there is hurt, bring healing. Where there is despair, bring hope. Where there is joy, bring strength. Where there is success, bring caution. Father speak to us from your Word today. Let us clearly hear from you. These things we ask in the name of Jesus Christ our Lord. **AMEN.**

Scriptures for personal meditation and reflection:

Jeremiah 9:1-26 : Psalm 136:1-26 : Luke 15:17

Personal Prayer Topics:

_____

_____

_____

_____

_____

_____

_____

_____

5.

O LORD OUR GOD, WE worship you this morning. We praise you that you are our Father and our God. You have shown yourself to us in so many different ways. We have experienced your love and power in the many and varied circumstances of our lives. Your presence with us has made all the difference to the outcome of our situations. We bless you this morning for the promises of your Word. They have been our strength and encouragement. They have been food for our faith. So this morning we bow our heads before you in worship. We lift up our hearts to you in praise. We would glorify your holy name.

Let us have a time for private prayer and reflection:

Father, as we come prayerfully before you, your Spirit searches our hearts and we know that we have failed you. We have said and done things that have pained your heart. Lord, forgive us we pray. Renew a right spirit within us. We acknowledge before you that at times we find it difficult to admit our failures and sin. Father, grant us your grace, so that we might reach out to you and receive from you the forgiveness and spiritual renewal that we so desperately need. May the blood of Jesus Christ your Son continue to cleanse us from all our sin.

We thank you Father that we can come into your presence and seek your searching of our souls. Diagnose the causes of our spiritual sickness. Perform the necessary remedial surgery. You are the Great Physician and Healer. You are able and willing and we thank you this morning for touching our lives and bringing us to that place where we can receive from you all that you want to give to us today. You alone are the One who can make us whole.

Lord God we pray this morning for . . . .

- All who serve others. We remember before you those who work in our hospitals - doctors and nurses, and the many staff members that make up the medical teams and support staff. Lord, we pray that the needs of people will always be uppermost in their minds. That you will give to them real compassion and care for those to whom they minister.

- Father, we pray for the economic situation of our world. It seems as though the poor countries get poorer and the rich get richer. Lord, we pray that you will move by your Spirit in the hearts of people in such a way that there is a re-evaluation of priorities. May values be reassessed, so that the needs of your world might be met.

- We pray for your Church that it might do your will; that in whatever situation your people find themselves, they may declare your love and power in their lives and many who have lost their way may be brought to you. Create strong leaders among your people, we pray. Endue them with your Spirit. Help them to make wise and right decisions in the continually changing circumstances of life.

So Lord, as we come to meditate on your Word this morning, help us to listen for your voice. May we heed the leading of your Spirit. May we be responsive to your call. Lord, we want our lives to count for you – so we ask that you will strengthen us and equip us through our worship today that we may be better prepared to live for you during this coming week. These things we ask in the name of Jesus Christ our Lord. **AMEN.**

Scriptures for private prayer and reflection:

Psalm 139 : 1 John 1:9

Personal Prayer Topics:

_____

_____

_____

_____

_____

_____

_____

6.

EAVENLY FATHER, WITH THE Psalmist of old, we say, "It is good to give thanks to the Lord, to sing praises to your name O Most High, to proclaim your steadfast love in the morning and your faithfulness at night". Lord, our hearts rejoice when we see your mighty acts and your steadfast love. Yours is the power and the glory O Lord, and we rejoice in your victory. We exalt your name together this morning, for you have done great things for us.

Lord, we thank you for the many personal blessings received this past week - for grace received in times of need - for strength imparted to us in moments of weakness - for ability bestowed that we might do Your will. We never cease to be amazed, O Lord, at the marvellous ways in which you meet us in the everyday affairs of life - in the office - on the shop floor - in the home - in the mall - in the school. You walk with us wherever we are. We just praise you today for your continued presence with us.

Let us have a time for private thanksgiving and reflection:

How often, our Father, we are insensitive to your presence. We become preoccupied with the things around us and lay ourselves open to temptation. Then we wonder why we fall! Lord, forgive us for our wilfulness and our disobedience to your Word. O God, it is so easy to focus on our own needs and be forgetful of others. We always know what we want, but we are not so aware of what others need. Forgive us, Lord, when we only concentrate on ourselves. Father, lift us out of ourselves and our preoccupation with our own concerns. Let us share your vision for the world and for your Church. Father, set us free from our small and limited visions. Release within us a new measure of faith. Awaken within us a renewed trust in your promises. So often, O Lord, we can only see things from where we are. Grant to us your perspective on life, so that we may serve you more effectively in the power of your Holy Spirit.

Lord we come before you to intercede for your world . . . . (Expand these topics)

- We pray for a spiritual awakening in . . . . (A nation, a city, an area of the world)
- We remember before you the Leaders of nations . . . . (Name some who are in the news)
- We pray for the missionary task force around the world.
- For any specific needs there may be in the community . . . .

Father, we want to hear your voice speaking to us today. Tune our hearts therefore to listen, and listening, may we obey your call. Strengthen and renew each one of us as we respond to you in worship and commitment. We ask this in the all powerful name of Jesus Christ our Lord. **AMEN.**

Scriptures for private prayer and reflection:

Psalm 92 : Psalm 100

Personal Prayer Topics:

_____

_____

_____

_____

_____

_____

_____

7.

O LORD OUR GOD, WE just rejoice in all you are doing. We just want to praise you today. You are eternally God. You never forget your covenant with your people and your promises are sure. Your steadfast love endures forever. We magnify your name this morning for your continual goodness towards us. You have saved us, upheld us and kept us. You have led us along sure and tested paths. You have delivered us in moments of temptation and given us victory through our Lord Jesus Christ. You provide for us in every way and we have been the glad recipients of your grace. So we praise you this morning.

Our Father, when "great things" come our way, it's comparatively easy to breathe our "thanks". But so often we let the "smaller things" slip by without showing our gratitude. So this morning we would thank you for the Christian kindness of friends.

We thank you for . . . .

- Those who have taken time to help us
- The daily provision of our needs which we often take for granted
- Those whom we have been able to help and encourage

- What we have learned when the way has been hard going

Above all, today we thank you for the Lord Jesus Christ in whom we live and move and have our being, and that with Him you have freely given us all that is needful to live for your praise and glory.

Introduce a moment or so of silent prayer by saying:

In the quietness of our own hearts let us thank God for those very personal blessings that God has given to us.

Father, as we walk in the light, we become increasingly aware of the darkness within and of those wrong things within us. So we come before you seeking that inner cleansing and forgiveness that only you can give. Forgive us Lord, when we hide behind words in order to cover up for our lack of experience of you. Forgive us for having higher standards for others than for ourselves. Forgive us for our pride which robs us of our humility. For every unworthy thought, for every unloving deed, for every thoughtless word that we have spoken, we ask your forgiveness. Forgive us also for our broken relationships and for the prejudice that enables us to see the faults in others yet keeps us blind to our own. Cleanse us from our sins we pray through the finished work of Jesus on the cross.

Lord God we would pray for . . . . (Expand these topics)

- World peace . . . . (Name any areas where there is conflict)
- Those who once professed to know you and now walk along different paths
- Our young people - that their idealism may find expression in true Christian living
- Overseas missions and missionaries . . . .

Gracious Father, may the fruit of your Spirit grow in our lives, so that Jesus may be more clearly seen in us. May your joy fill our hearts and lives and be our daily strength. Give us, we pray, patience in service and a continual willingness to learn. Minister to us now from your Word. This we ask in Jesus' name. **AMEN**.

Scriptures for private prayer and reflection:

Psalm 9:1-20 : Psalm 146 : John 6:60-71 : Romans 10:1-15 Ephesians 2:1-10

Personal Prayer Topics:

_____

_____

_____

_____

_____

_____

_____

8.

FATHER, WE ARE SO delighted to be in your presence this morning. The fact that you want us to come to you like this, gives us such confidence. Everything around us this morning speaks of your loving kindness. You have provided for our needs. You have comforted us in our sorrows and disappointments. You have encouraged us when the way has been hard. We just want to praise you this morning for the grace that we have experienced in our lives. We praise you that the impossible is perfectly possible with you. We worship you this morning because you have revealed your love to us in the Lord Jesus Christ and enabled us to experience it through faith in Him. Lord, we ask that you will accept the praise and worship of our hearts.

Gracious God, when we think of the great variety of your gifts to us, that come fresh every morning, we are so grateful. In particular we thank you for the gift of your Spirit. He assists us when the way is hard. He is our Teacher in spiritual things. He makes the Lord Jesus real to our hearts and He enables us to pray effectively. Lord, for the wonderful gift of yourself to us in the person of your Spirit we offer you our thanks today. Without Him, O Lord, our faith would be an ineffective philosophy and our highest ideals and obedience to your will would be completely unattainable. For all your Spirit means to us as individuals and as a church we give you our thanks.

Let us silently reflect on God's goodness and grace:

Yet, our Father, we must confess there are times when we frustrate the work of your Spirit. We resist His leading. We shut our eyes to the challenge He presents to us and we shut our ears to His voice. Forgive us O Lord, that in spite of the fact that we have experienced so much of your goodness, we still struggle to go our own way. Sometimes, O Lord, our own behaviour baffles us. Father, please forgive us for any ill will that we may have borne towards others or created for others - for any unworthy thoughts that we have entertained and even cherished. Forgive us, Lord, that every time you ask us to do something, we automatically find an excuse for not wanting to do it. Father, we lay out our sins before you this morning and ask that you will forgive us and fill us anew with your Holy Spirit, in order that holiness may more readily characterise our lives.

Father we again pray for your world of which we are a part . . . .
(Expand these topics)

- For our own nation, Lord, forgive us for . . . . (Name any national sins), help us to see that sin is a reproach to any people and that righteousness alone can exalt a nation.
- For your Church around the world that it may meet the challenges of the hour . . . .
- For the effectiveness of the witness of individual Christians in their place of work, in their homes, at school and college.
- For all missionary outreach through radio and television and through the internet
- For the situation in . . . . (For some emergency, crisis or difficulty)

Apart from you, O Lord, we amount to nothing. Help us therefore to feed on the Bread of Life. Make us hungry and thirsty for spiritual things. As we meditate on your Word today satisfy our spiritual longings we pray. Lord we have great expectations of you today. Hear our prayer as we offer it in the name of Jesus Christ our Lord and Saviour. **AMEN.**

Scriptures for private prayer and reflection:

Psalm 23 : Hebrews 4:16 : Hebrews 10:19-25 : Hebrews 13:5-8

Personal Prayer Topics:

_____

_____

_____

_____

_____

_____

_____

9.

LORD OUR GOD, THE theme of our lives will always be your marvellous works and the glory and splendour of your majesty. Week by week and day by day we view your mighty acts with awe and wonder. As we worship, we recite the story of your abounding goodness and sing of your righteousness. Father, you are gracious and compassionate at all times, even in judgement. There's never a moment when your promises fail to materialize. You are unchanging in all your ways. So we lift up our voices in praise to you today.

We give you thanks O Lord that you are near to all who sincerely call on you. You are only a prayer away! We thank you that you watch over all who love you. Lord when we think of you our hearts echo the words of the Psalmist who said, "Every day will I bless you and extol your name forever and ever". Thank you Lord for all of your guidance over this past week; for every revelation of yourself that has come to us from your Word. We thank you for the working of your Holy Spirit within our hearts, sanctifying us and making us useable in the Master's service.

CONVERSATIONS WITH GOD

Let us have a time for private prayer and reflection:

Gracious God, if you kept account of our sins and held them against us, we would not be able to hold up our heads in your presence. We would have to hide our faces from you in shame. But in you O Lord, forgiveness is to be found and so we come to you to acknowledge our sins and failures. Lord, how often we judge others by your standards and ourselves by our own.

Father forgive us we pray. We confess O Lord, there are times when we go through the motions of faith, yet our hearts are empty and a sense of unreality paralyses us. Please forgive us. Pardon us we pray, for relying so much on our own insight and logical deductions and not on the leading of your Spirit and the clear instructions of your Word. For our failures in the hour of temptation and for our lack of faith to draw on your resources that would have made victory certain, we ask your forgiveness. By our sins we have marred your image in us and robbed you of glory. Cleanse us from every stain of sin through the sacrifice of Jesus on the cross. Clothe us we pray in His righteousness and heal the brokenness of our lives. We thank you for the assurance of forgiveness that if we confess our sins, you are just and will forgive us our sins and cleanse us from all unrighteousness.

Father we come before you to intercede on behalf of . . . . (Expand these topics)

- Those who feel their lives are falling apart under the strains and stresses of life
- Those who are seeking you but as yet have not found you
- Those that administer our schools and colleges and universities
- Those who have a genuine concern for the world in which we live, yet do not know the real solution to its problems

- Those who are carrying heavy burdens of . . . . (Name them as appropriate)
- Those who are involved in the ministry of evangelism at home and overseas – (Name any evangelists that are known – any special missions that are underway)

Father, ignite the flame of love within our hearts and may it burn brightly for your glory. May your Holy Spirit empower us day by day so that we may be your witnesses. Please keep us faithful in prayer. Do not allow anything to disrupt our communication with you. In the changing spheres of life, may our loyalty to you be unquestionable. So may your Word minister to us today and achieve your purposes in our lives. This we ask through Jesus Christ our Lord. **AMEN.**

Scriptures for private prayer and reflection:

Psalm 145 : Romans 2:1-16 : Ephesians 1:3-2:10
Philippians 4:12-13

Personal Prayer Topics:

_____

_____

_____

_____

_____

_____

_____

10.

O LORD OUR GOD, YOU have been the safe and secure dwelling place of your people in every generation. You have encouraged us to rest on you and we do so because there is nowhere else to go. We acknowledge before you that all the treasures of wisdom and knowledge are to be found in you. So Lord, we praise and magnify your holy name. We rejoice together today in your salvation. We never cease to be amazed that you set your love on us and redeemed us through the shed blood of your Son the Lord Jesus Christ and that you have given to us the gift of your holy and magnificent Spirit. We praise you this morning for all your mighty acts.

Gracious God, we thank you that you are like a father to us. None of our needs are too small or too large for you to meet. We thank you for the encouragement you give us through the Scriptures to exercise childlike faith and trust in you. We know that you are the same yesterday, today and forever. You never change towards us your people. We thank you therefore that we can boldly approach you with our requests. We thank you that through the death and resurrection of our Lord Jesus Christ, we have access to all the resources of heaven. For all your many mercies to us day by day, accept our thanks.

Let us come before the Lord in silent adoration:

Father how often we cut ourselves off from your blessings and make our prayers null and void because we allow sin free rein in our lives. Often O Lord we allow unforgiving attitudes and lack of love to go unconfessed and uncorrected. For this we ask your forgiveness.

We recognise too that often our service for you counts for nothing because we forget what you have told us - that if we have anything against our brother, we should first put this right before we come and make our offering of worship and service to you. Forgive us Lord, that our faith is so small and that we limit you by our sheer unbelief. Help us not to substitute common sense for the leading of your Spirit. Deliver us, Father, from our doubting and enable us by your grace to take you at your Word and to trust you to the end. Grant that we may never be afraid to claim your promises and in doing so may we glorify your name.

Father we pray for . . . . (Expand these topics)

- Those who are imprisoned for their faith in the Lord Jesus . . . .
- The vast continent of South America - for continued openness to the Gospel and that you O Lord would stabilise the very delicate balance of power . . . .
- Community and religious leaders . . . .
- Any who this morning may have very specific needs . . . .
- Young people that they will have openness to the Gospel . . . .
- The sick and those who are in hospital . . . (Names could be mentioned here with the person's permission)
- Those that are feeling the limitations of their age . . . .

As we turn to your Word this morning, open our eyes to see your truth. Enable us to focus on those things that you have for us. Father, we want to see Jesus. Grant to us therefore the desire of our hearts, for we ask for His name's sake. **AMEN.**

Scriptures for private prayer and reflection:

Psalm 46 : Luke 15:1-7 : Romans 8:28-39

Personal Prayer Topics:

_____

_____

_____

_____

_____

_____

_____

11.

O LORD OUR GOD THERE is no one like you. You have set your throne on high and surrounded yourself with the glory and majesty of heaven. Angels just delight to do your will. Yet O Lord you are concerned about us in our need. You lift up the weak. You raise the fallen. You restore the broken, bestowing on them unspeakable blessings and privileges. You are like a father to us and we praise you. We bless you O Lord, that you have placed a measure of faith in us, to entrust us with the Gospel and its proclamation. O God our Father, the splendour of your Word, the magnitude of your promises, and the ability of your Spirit just leaves us in awe and wonder. Humbly we bow before you now in worship and praise.

We thank you Lord that your hand has been on us for good during this past week. Your care for us shows itself in so many unexpected ways. Even when we resisted your entrance into our circumstances, you found a way to help us, in spite of our stubbornness. We thank you for the practical Christian fellowship that you have given to us, that has supported us and encouraged us. Father, we just thank you this morning that you match your grace to our many and devious ways. Father, accept the praise and gratitude that we bring to you now.

Father we desire more than anything else this morning, that more of Jesus could be seen and experienced in our lives. Often O Lord, we make the way harder for others to follow you because of how we live. We acknowledge before you O Lord, that often in our relationships we are deficient in love and understanding. In our work we are grudging and half-hearted.

For this, Father, we seek your forgiveness this morning. We confess O Lord that at times we find ourselves questioning your goodness and doubting your love. We allow resentment and bitterness to poison our attitudes. We allow our thoughts and intentions to become unruly. Gracious God, in response to the confession of our hearts today, bestow on us your forgiveness we pray. Help us to realise afresh that Jesus died to set us free from the rule of sin, and rose again to impart to us His eternal life and all the resources of heaven.

Father we come before you in intercession for: . . . . (Expand these topics)

- The elderly who are feeling their limitations . . . .
- Our young people who sense the breathlessness of our modern world . . . .
- Those who have lost their way through life . . . .
- Those unable to be in worship today because of their work . . . . (Name some professions)
- Those in our families and among our friends who do not know you personally . . . .
- Those whose lives are oppressed by Satan and have almost lost hope . . . .

Gracious Father, help us to submit to the rule of your Spirit within our hearts. Grant us the courage to act on our convictions as we meditate on your Word. Enable us by your grace to fulfil the visions that circulate in our minds and Father, when the way gets tough, grant that we shall be able to give you praise. This we ask through Jesus Christ our Lord and King. **AMEN.**

Scriptures for private prayer and reflection:

Genesis 15:20 : 2 Corinthians 9:8 and 12:9

Personal Prayer Topics:

_____

_____

_____

_____

_____

_____

_____

12.

O LORD OUR GOD, AS we pause before you during this time of worship, we acknowledge that we don't always find it easy to pray. So often we become preoccupied with our own inner thoughts and struggles. The things that we have forgotten suddenly come back to mind and form a spiritual smoke screen. Father, we find it so hard to focus our thoughts on you because of the numerous things that begin to fill our minds when we are still in your presence. Yet O Lord, we are confident this morning, that you understand us. You have walked this earth. You have felt the pull of temptation. You have felt the pressure of the busyness of the world around. So Lord, we draw near to worship you. Enable us Father, by the power of your Spirit, to rise above these things that would seek to distract us from worshipping you. Fire our hearts we pray with new devotion. Release within us your love, so that we might be caught up in heart to heart fellowship with you.

We thank you Lord, for your patience with us. You never give up on us. You constantly nudge us by your Spirit, through your Word, so that we might walk in your ways. We thank you for making us members of your family; for giving to us eternal life; for extending to us your forgiveness. We thank you for the gift of your indwelling Spirit to equip and guide us through our day to day lives. We thank you for your church and the mutual strengthening that is gained by being part of it. For the fellowship and worship that we enjoy together today, we thank you.

Our lives are open to you, as we come before you this morning. There is nothing that is hidden from your eyes. In one sense O Lord, this is encouraging because we know that you are aware of all the "ups and downs" of our lives. But it is also disquieting because sometimes we want to keep things hidden from you and from others. We confess O Lord, that there is something within us that wants to make us hide our sins rather than confess them to you. So Lord we bow before you this morning, not so much with a willingness of spirit but with a determination of heart to do the right thing and to acknowledge our shortcomings before you. Father, you know how much we need the ministry of your Spirit within our hearts, to forgive our sins, to heal our hurts, to bring wholeness to our brokenness. As we open our hearts to you now in the quietness of this place, minister your renewing grace to us, we pray.

Let's have a few moments of silent prayer and reflection:

Gracious God, once again we thank you for the privilege of being able to pray for others.

We remember before you . . . . (Expand these topics)

- Our families and those members who live and work in other countries . . . . that . . . .
- The homes and families in our community . . . .
- The broken hearted who feel that their world has been shattered . . . .
- The discouraged who find it difficult to exercise any faith or hope . . . .

- The lonely that crave contact with other people . . . .
- Those serving you overseas on the mission field. We bring before you . . . .

Mighty God you have brought us together this morning for a purpose. You desire that our lives reflect your glory. As we meditate on your Word, may your truth sanctify our hearts and prepare us for the challenges that face us during this coming week. Help us to be truly your disciples. We ask this in the name of Jesus Christ our Sovereign Lord. **AMEN.**

Scriptures for private prayer and reflection:

Nehemiah 9:17 : Matthew 28:19-20 : John 20:21

Personal Prayer Topics:

_____

_____

_____

_____

_____

_____

_____

13.

O LORD OUR GOD, WHAT a wonderful God you are. Who can ever compare with you? You are sovereign in power. You are supreme in love and holiness. Yet the amazing thing is that you reach out to us in mercy and grace in the Lord Jesus Christ and invite us to come to you. You said, "Come to me all you who are weary and burdened and I will give you rest". We praise you for your gift of salvation that delivers us from sin and grants us inner peace and eternal life. We worship you Lord for the gift of your powerful Spirit that you have placed within your people. When our minds begin to focus on you O Lord, we find ourselves lost in wonder, love and praise.

Father, we are thankful that you have been with us during this past week. You have supplied all our needs. You have very wonderfully provided for us in every way. We thank you that we have never been alone because you have been by our side. We give you our thanks for your Word and for the faith to believe it and the strength to obey it. When we have prayed you have answered us. Sometimes you have said "no" and we haven't always appreciated it. Sometimes you have said "wait" and our patience has been severely tested. Many times you have said "yes" and we have rejoiced in your goodness. Sometimes Lord we find it hard to say thank you, but even so our hearts warm to you with a deep sense of gratitude this morning. As the hymn writer says, "God moves in mysterious ways, His wonders to perform". We just thank you that you are always active on our behalf, even when we can't see or understand what you are doing.

Let's pause for a moment of quiet reflection and confession:

Only when we come into your presence Father, and listen to your Word, do we realise the extent of our sin and the constant need we have of your grace and forgiveness. So often O Lord, we play with temptation and then wonder why we fall for it. Lord grant us forgiveness and the faith to believe that you can deliver us. Father, we confess before you our inconsistency of life. When we look at the Lord Jesus He is always constant in His attitude towards us and towards others. Lord make us more like Jesus, as you extend your forgiveness to us. Father forgive us that we are so often prepared to live with a sense of unreality in our souls and not do anything about it. O God, lead us to that point where we can have a more significant fellowship with you. Forgive us Father, for our lack of positive witness and distinctive Christian service. We confess that often we get very busy and achieve very little. Help us to evaluate our work in the light of your Word and grant us the courage to eliminate those things that do not promote your Kingdom or glorify your name.

Father this morning we pray for . . . . (Expand these topics)

- Those who are sick . . . . those in hospital . . . . those waiting to go into hospital
- Those who have suffered loss through bereavement, divorce or separation . . . .
- Those who are over burdened by the pressures of life . . . .
- Those who feel trapped by the circumstances of their lives . . . .

- The proclamation of the Gospel through Christian writers and actors . . . .

Gracious God open our eyes to your truth this morning as we study your Word. Enable us to apply in our lives what you are saying to us. As a result, may our lives demonstrate the reality and power of the Lord Jesus. So mould our characters after the pattern of your will. This we ask in the name of Jesus Christ our Lord. **AMEN.**

Scriptures for private prayer and reflection:

2 Samuel 12:1-14 : Psalm 9:1-20 : Psalm 103:1-22

Personal Prayer Topics:

_____

_____

_____

_____

_____

_____

14.

*L*ORD GOD HOW GREAT and marvellous you are. In your great wisdom you created the world. Day by day you sustain it by your mighty power. When your world was marred by sin you planned its redemption through the death and resurrection of our Lord Jesus Christ. Father, we praise you for all your mighty acts. Although you are exalted on high and have a universe to take care of, you still make yourself available to us. You are never too busy to listen to us and to deal with the concerns that we bring you. So Father, we come into your presence this morning, knowing that you reward those who seek you.

Gracious God, we know that every blessing we have comes from your hand. You have told us in your Word that you will not withhold any good thing from those who love you. We give you our thanks, for the teaching of your Word and the leading of your Spirit. Father we thank you that when we pause to meditate on your Word and talk with you in prayer that you are there to meet with us. We are so grateful that you are never a disappointment to your people.

Let us have a time of silence for personal confession:

Lord God, you know how often we try to live the Christian life by relying on our own strength. We try to generate our own enthusiasm. We try to regulate our service. We add conditions to our love. Forgive us Lord, when we try to bargain with you; when we fail to live our lives by faith and trust in you. As we look at your holiness and perfection, we realise how imperfect our lives really are. We think of those occasions when we have spoken hastily, when we have passed off half-truths as the whole truth. We pray for your forgiveness. Sometimes it amazes us how easily we slip back into our old ways that are so dishonouring to you and disfiguring to our Christian testimony. Father, how much we miss out on, because of our unbelief. So often because of our lack of consecration we put ourselves in the place where we cannot be used by you. Forgive us Father, we so often rob you of your glory and bring dishonour to your name. Equip us to serve you in the Kingdom into which you have brought us.

Lord God this morning we pray for . . . . (Expand these topics)

- All those who serve you on the mission field. Particularly we remember . . . . (Here you can insert the names of people working in different spheres)
- Those responsible for the production and distribution of Christian literature . . . .
- Those engaged in medical work in your name . . . .
- Our nation - our province / state - our city . . . .
- Those who are captive to some habit, attitude, or wrong relationship . . . .
- Those who have rejected you because of some unfortunate encounter with your Church in earlier years . . . .

Today O Lord, we pray that we may learn greater dependence on you. Help us to be better witnesses to your saving grace. So Lord, lead us into a fuller knowledge of your will and may we have the grace to obey it. We ask all these things in the precious name of Jesus Christ our Lord. **AMEN**

Scriptures for private prayer and reflection:

2 Corinthians 1:3-4 : Matthew 23:1-12 : Mark 10:35-45

Personal Prayer Topics:

_____

_____

_____

_____

_____

_____

_____

15.

SENSE OF EXCITEMENT FILLS our hearts today as we bow before you in prayer. We are coming to the One whose love and kindness is beyond measure and whose faithfulness towers above the earth like a beacon. Your glory is matchless. You have made wonderful promises to us which you always honour. You have made available to us all the rich resources of heaven. The daily miracles that you perform demonstrate your goodness and declare your glory and majesty. Everything that you do O God is just and good and all your laws are right and designed for our happiness and your glory. Father, in the spirit of togetherness we just want to express our praise to you this morning.

Thank you for bringing us together today. Thank you too, for the way in which you have been active in the circumstances of our lives this week. We have drawn on your guidance. We have proved the reliability of your Word. We have had the joy of the Lord in our hearts and it has proved to be our strength. For these and all your other gifts to us, accept our thanks. Father, we would not voice our thanks to you as a mere duty, but out of our experience of your love and mercy towards us. Lord we love you because you first loved us. Please accept the thanks that we express to you this morning.

Father, as we bow our heads in your holy presence, our prayer is that of the Psalmist who said, "Search me O God, and know my heart; test my thoughts; point out anything that you find in me that makes you sad; and lead me along the path of everlasting life". We confess O Lord that life becomes so burdensome under the pressure of sin. So often we try to forget about it or we try to live with it, when really we ought to confess it to you, so that the weight can be lifted from us. Lord, this is what you want and have promised to do. Forgive us Lord, for not taking you at your Word and just relying on our own wisdom. Father, how soon we forget about the gracious ways in which you deal with us. We have such short memories when it comes to what you have done for us. Lord God, cleanse from our hearts any bitterness or resentment that may be poisoning our relationships with others and with you. Enable us to mend any broken relationships. Father as we draw near to the cross this morning, in response to our confession of need, grant us the knowledge of sins forgiven and the inward assurance that our lives have the stamp of your approval on them.

We come before you in intercession today for . . . . (Expand these topics)

- Those trouble spots in our world . . . . (Name the places)
- Those who have been married in this church over the last year . . . .
- Those in bondage to fear and the fruits of past living . . . .
- Our young people who are away at college and university . . . . (Names of students)
- Those who do not know you as Lord and Saviour . . . .
- The different departments of our church life . . . . (Focus on one specific area)

Gracious God, fill us anew with your Holy Spirit. Enrich our lives by your indwelling presence. Grant us the grace to trust you more. Give to us we pray that faith that is able to move mountains. Speak to us today, not just in the way we want, but according to our real needs.

Lord, minister to us from your Word. We ask this in the all powerful name of Jesus Christ our Lord. **AMEN**

Scriptures for private prayer and meditation:

Psalm 126:1-6 : Ephesians 4:1-16 : Philippians 1:1-11

Personal Prayer Topics:

_____

_____

_____

_____

_____

_____

_____

16.

GOD OUR FATHER, YOUR people have proclaimed your praises for generations. We would add our voices to theirs, declaring that you are worthy of praise and the allegiance of our hearts. We come before you humbled by the fact that you love us, unworthy as we are. We are so grateful that you have not dealt with us according to what we deserve, but according to your great mercy and love. Father, we worship and adore you, for you are our Saviour and Redeemer. Lord, we bless you that you desire to dwell in us and express your life through us and that you challenge us to make you our dwelling place. We cannot come before you without expressing our thanks to you. You have brought us to this point in time. You have kept us steadfast by your power. Your love is like a bird hovering over us. Thank you Lord, for being our Heavenly Father and including us in your royal family. Gracious God, we cherish every thought of you and your Word to us is precious. Please accept the thanks of a grateful people this morning.

Let us have a time of silence for private thanksgiving and reflection:

Forgive us, Lord, if we have become preoccupied with our own failures and not enough with your grace that is adequate for our every need. We know Father, that apart from you we can do nothing of lasting worth. Yet Lord, how hard we try to assert ourselves and be something in our own right. Forgive us Father, when we glory in the gifts that you have given to us and do not give due recognition to their source and inspiration. How we must grieve you by our waywardness. Yet O Lord, you keep your strong arms around us, upholding us in our weakness, protecting us in moments when we are particularly vulnerable to the Evil One. Father as we look back over our shoulders we can see that you have been steering our lives. Even though we have made many mistakes, you have woven them into your instructive purpose, and have made all things work together for good. Lord, forgive us for our little faith, and our lack of trust in you when things haven't gone exactly as we would have wished. Cleanse us, renew us, strengthen us and reassure us that we are yours. Lord God, grant us we pray, truthfulness of speech, integrity of action and holiness of character.

Father we intercede for . . . . (Expand these topics)

- Those who feel confused as they think of the future . . . .
- Those that feel hurt, broken and maybe forgotten . . . .
- Those who feel so ordinary, they wonder if you really have a purpose for them in life
- Those in management and unions as they seek to lead and relate to one another . . . .
- Those who seek to maintain law and order in our society and for the police in our own community . . . .
- Those that hold the lives of others in their hands in the decisions that they make, in the actions they advocate, and in the words that they speak . . . .

Lord God, let us hear something directly from you this morning. A word that will put new heart into us and enable us to face all the varied pressures that life will bring to us. This we ask in our Saviour and Redeemer's name. **AMEN.**

Scriptures for private prayer and reflection:

1 Chronicles 16:4-36 : Psalm 92:1-15 : Philippians 1:1-21

Personal Prayer Topics:

_____

_____

_____

_____

_____

_____

_____

17.

GOD OUR FATHER, WE praise you that you are the very foundation of our lives. We affirm this morning that our lives are built on you. When that gnawing question "why" arises in our minds, you speak your words of peace to our troubled lives. Father, we want to magnify your name today because of all that we have received from you. It is so reassuring to know that we are in your hands and that you will never let us go. Gracious God, you are our security in these changing times and in this certainty we rejoice today. You are our refuge and strength.

Father, we thank you for your enduring patience with us. Even when we are forgetful of you, you remember us and quietly minister to us through your Holy Spirit and through the Scriptures. We thank you too for those little correctional nudges that you give to us, so that we might stay on course. We thank you that there can be no pretending when we come into your presence. We thank you that you have delivered us from the bondage of outward show, even though at times it clings closely to us.

Lord God, as we come before you we long for a fuller measure of your Holy Spirit in our lives. We desire those strong wings of faith that we might rise to the spiritual heights that you have set for us. Forgive us Father that we are so slow to trust you and become so easily satisfied with ourselves. As we come into your presence this morning, we recognise the subtlety of sin as it creeps through our lives. Root it out, we pray. Cleanse us through the shed blood of Jesus Christ. Renew us in the Holy Spirit and empower us for your service. Restore to us the joy of our salvation.

Lord God we come to you on behalf of others. We pray for . . . .
(Expand these topics)

- Those who are in hospital and those family members who are anxious . . . .
- Those whom we love who do not yet know you . . . .
- Those who seek to corrupt and pervert our society . . . .
- Church leaders throughout the world and our own denominational leaders . . . .
- Our nation . . . . (Name any particular issue that is of concern)

Let us have a time of silent prayer to bring personal needs to the Lord:

Lord, you know our hopes and fears and so we bring them to you. You know our questing after truth and the problems we encounter along the way. At times it seems as though there is no God. We get discouraged and feel depressed. Yet we know that standing somewhere in the shadows is Jesus. Therefore, Lord as we focus on your Word this morning, give us a real sense of your presence, enliven our worship, strengthen our witness and equip us for your work. This we ask through Jesus Christ our Lord. **AMEN**

Scriptures for private prayer and reflection:

Luke 15:11-22 : Romans 5:1-11 : 2 Thessalonians 1:1-12

Personal Prayer Topics:

_____

_____

_____

_____

_____

_____

_____

18.

*L*ORD, WE BEGIN THIS day with rejoicing. We acknowledge that you are a wonderful God. Nothing is impossible to you. You nurture us with your love and care. Day by day you reveal yourself to us in your Word. We see your hand in the events of our daily lives. We are amazed at the strength you give to us that enables us to stand when everyone else is crumbling. Our whole world is full of your glory. But we see your glory the clearest in our Lord Jesus Christ before whom we bow this morning in awe and wonder and in thankfulness and praise.

We thank you, Lord, for the sheer joy of knowing you. Without you we could not go on for another day. We thank you for your abiding friendship towards us. You do everything to draw us into a closer walk with yourself. We thank you for the fellowship of your church and for the strength and comfort that we derive from it. We thank you for the gift of Christian people to us. They encourage us. They build us up as they utilize the gifts you have given them. They challenge us to greater endeavour. They rebuke us when we need correction. They love us when everyone else deserts us. They affirm us when we feel so unworthy. We offer our thanks to you this morning as part of our worship.

Let us have a time of silent prayer to offer our personal thanks to God:

Lord God, you know our hearts – the burdens we carry – the secrets that are locked up within us – the fears that we dare not voice in case we are misunderstood. Father, we would release our hold on these things and give them over to you this morning. We cast our cares on you because we know that you care about us. Lord, so often we allow such things to rob us of our peace, because we will not relinquish our hold upon them. We feel that we must hold on to them or they will get out of control. We feel an inner pressure to try to resolve these things on our own. Father, forgive us for our lack of trust and confidence in you. Lord, renew our faith in your ability to be the solution to our deepest needs. For some of us, our hearts are filled with joy and we are tasting victory and achievement. We feel as though we have the world by the tail! Grant that in the midst of all this we may not become forgetful of you. Lord, we pray, enter into our joys and successes and add to them new heights and depths and in so doing bring glory to your name.

Lord God we come before you in intercession for . . . . (Expand these topics)

- All those who suffer at the hands of their fellow men . . . .
- Our students as they face examinations and have to make career choices . . . .
- Those churches that are in rural areas that they may minister in the power of your Spirit and be encouraged by what they see you doing . . . .
- Those who are "shut-in" and unable to get out to worship and have no fellowship with other believers . . . .
- Those that are deaf and blind and find communication difficult . . . .

O Lord our God, grant us a greater capacity to love you and to love one another. Pour your Spirit of power into our hearts. May our worship be a true expression of the thoughts of our heart. Instruct us through the preaching of your Word today that we may grow in grace and in our knowledge of you. This we ask through our Lord Jesus Christ. **AMEN**

Scriptures for private prayer and reflection:

Mark 4:35-41 : Acts 1:1-11

Personal Prayer Topics:

_____

_____

_____

_____

_____

_____

_____

19.

ATHER, WE HAVE COME here this morning to meet with you. We have an appointment with you. We come therefore expecting that our time together will be profitable in every way. Just to think that you want to have fellowship with us is an incredible thought. It humbles us and at the same time excites us. We do love you Lord and desire with all our hearts to get to know you better. We are amazed at the limitless resources of grace that you have made available to us. How rich we are! We have confidence in you today because we know that you will never turn us away. You will never turn a deaf ear to our heartfelt prayers. Father, what a wonder you are! We worship you! We adore you! We love you!

Unworthy as we are, we thank you that in our Lord Jesus Christ you have clothed us with His righteousness. We thank you that you have transferred us from the Kingdom of Darkness to the Kingdom of Light. Lord, you redeemed us for yourself and placed your Spirit within us. For every victory won, for every encouragement received, we offer you our thanks today. We thank you for this time of corporate worship, when all the members of your family can come together in this place and offer you praise without any fear of persecution.

Let us have a time for silent reflection and personal thanksgiving:

Father, as conscious as we are of your love and grace towards us, we are also aware of the wrong within us. Many things, at times, block our fellowship with you and with one another. How easy it is for resentments locked within our hearts to stop the work of your Spirit in us. How easy it is for bitterness and lack of love to form a barrier between you and us. Forgive us Lord, we pray. So often, Father, we lack trust in you and we try to muddle through life in our own strength. Even the gifts that you give to us we misuse. Lord, we are so undeserving of your mercy yet you extend it to us in your Son. Father, forgive us, when we stand in the way of you blessing others. Gracious God, may we ever realise that all sin, however we may classify it, is sin against you. So this morning we ask that you will cleanse us from all known sin and renew a right spirit within us. We believe your Word that tells us that there is now no condemnation to those who are in right fellowship with the Lord Jesus Christ.

Father, when we come into your presence, we think not only of ourselves but we also want to share with you our concerns for others.

We bring to you . . . . (Expand these topics)

- Those that lack the basic necessities of life - food, clothing, medical attention - and for all those who seek to minister to their needs . . . .
- All world leaders - remembering that "Righteousness exalts a nation but sin is a reproach to any people." . . . .
- Those that are denied justice and as a consequence are suffering . . . .
- Those involved in the ministry of outreach in your church . . . . (Name the people involved)

- Those involved in Christian film and video production . . . .
- Those involved in church leadership around the world . . . .

Minister to us this morning according to our needs and not necessarily in the way we ask, for we have a way O Lord, of overlooking essentials and holding on to things that we should let go. Sanctify us by your Spirit and empower us for your service in the world and in your church. This we ask through Jesus Christ our Lord. **AMEN**

Scriptures for private prayer and reflection:

Psalm 97:1-12 : Galatians 5:13-26 : Romans 12

Personal Prayer Topics:

_____

_____

_____

_____

_____

_____

_____

20.

THERE ARE TIMES, O Lord, when we feel as though we can't handle any more change. Standards are changing. Values are altering. People don't remain the same towards us. All of this change makes us feel very insecure and sometimes afraid. We are so grateful that you are the unchanging God. As your Word tells us, you are the same yesterday, today and forever. You are our refuge in the hurricanes of life. You are our anchor when the waves buffet us. You are our security when everything is in a state of flux. We praise you today, that we can count on you in every circumstance of our lives. We praise you that you are a God of mercy and grace. You don't deal with us according to what we deserve but according to your love and mercy. Father, if it wasn't for you we wouldn't be here today. We would be living a very different lifestyle. We thank you so much for your gift of new life to us. It never ceases to amaze us that you take the raw material of our lives and turn it into something of beauty and strength that reflects your glory. What a great God you are. We lift up our hearts to you and worship you.

Let us have a time of silent, prayerful reflection on - the grace of God:

When we compare ourselves to others around us, sometimes we can deceive ourselves as to the quality of our own goodness. It is only when we stand in your holy presence that we see ourselves in a true light. Forgive us, Father, that we spend so little time seeking your will for our lives. We recognise its importance but somehow other things can so easily crowd it out. Lord, we are more sensitive than we realize. We so easily hurt one another and in so doing hurt ourselves; sometimes by our thoughtless words; sometimes by our actions; and sometimes by omitting to do the right things. Forgive us we pray! We confess O Lord that we can slip into the rut of going through the motions of spiritual life, when in fact deadness and unreality fill our hearts. Sometimes, O God, we treat the church as though it were ours and not yours. We manipulate. We put pressure on others. We get angry when things don't work out the way we want them to. We scheme and plan as though the Holy Spirit were absent. Father, forgive us and fashion our lives after that of the Lord Jesus.

Father, you are Sovereign in this world. You govern this world's affairs. Therefore we come to you and ask that you will demonstrate your love and power in the lives of those for whom we pray and in those situations that we lift up to you now.

We pray for . . . . (Expand these topics)

- Satan's plans to be frustrated both in the Church and in the nation and in individual lives . . . .
- Our denominational / Church leadership . . . .
- Those seeking to proclaim your gospel in the inner cities . . . .
- Those involved in the ministry of music within the church . . . .
- Any situation that is making news in the media . . . .
  (Name it)
- The many homeless youth in our cities and those who work among them . . . .

- Any outreach ministries of our church . . . . (Name them with their specific needs)
- Those who seek to reach people for Christ through Internet chat rooms . . . .

As we focus on your Word this morning, build into us new spiritual strength so that we might stand firm in our changing world. Satisfy the longings of our hearts we pray, so that we may wholeheartedly devote ourselves to your service. Father, may miracles take place within our lives this morning. May our prejudices be removed. May our hardness be softened; may our blindness be replaced by sight. This we ask through Jesus Christ our Lord and King. **AMEN.**

Scriptures for private prayer and reflection:

Exodus 14:1-31 : Matthew 16:21-28 : John 2:1-11

Personal Prayer Topics:

_____

_____

_____

_____

_____

_____

21.

RACIOUS GOD, IT'S SO thrilling to see what you are doing in our lives and in the lives of our fellow believers. The changes are just remarkable. The vision that you give and the strength imparted to fulfil it is almost unbelievable. You have brought us from spiritual death to life and we praise your holy name. We are absolutely amazed at what we can achieve with your strength. Things that were thought to be impossible have been brought within our reach. How good you are to us! We praise you for sending Jesus into the world to be our Saviour from sin's destructive power; to be our shelter in desperate hours and to be our security in the changing seasons of life. We find it very difficult at times to frame adequate words to express what is really in our hearts. You are wonderfully precious to us. The ways in which your grace touches our lives goes beyond our wildest dreams. We love you, Lord, with all our heart.

Let us have a time of silent prayer and reflection:

You have told us in your Word, to come boldly to your Throne of Grace. Sometimes, O Lord, that is more difficult than it sounds. At times our sins and failures overwhelm us. Our sense of guilt paralyses us. Father, we seek your forgiveness and cleansing this morning. Give to us, we pray, clean hands and pure hearts, so that we may stand in your presence with confidence of spirit and joy in our innermost being. Forgive us, Father, that we have such short memories. We forget the many things you have done in our lives. We forget the gracious way that you have dealt with us. Lord we admit to our shame that sometimes we live as though you were not there! When we think about it, it sends shivers down our spine. Our own behaviour baffles us at times. We thank you Lord, that you understand us because you created us. Therefore you minister to us in ways that we are able to understand. The wonder of your forgiveness still puzzles us, but nonetheless we rejoice in it. It is our only hope as we stand before a holy God. Release us we pray from the power and stain of sin. Enable us to rejoice in our new found liberty. Help us, O God, to be ready to extend our forgiveness to others, remembering that unless we do, you will not forgive us. May we ever be ready to let the love you have placed within our hearts cover the sins of others. Make us, we pray, your ministers of reconciliation among the people around us.

Father, when you have cleansed our hearts and renewed our spirits we see your world quite differently. We become burdened by the things which are of concern to you. We begin to feel, in some measure, as you feel about your world.

So Lord, we come and intercede for . . . . (Expand these topics)

- The opening of the eyes of those who are spiritually blind . . . .
- The removal of the cloud of boredom that rests over so many people's lives today . . . .
- Those that are experiencing acute loneliness on account of divorce or separation or bereavement . . . .
- The single people in our fellowship that you will minister to their specific needs . . . .

- The youth of our church and all the potential that is wrapped up in every life . . . .
- The different women's ministries in our church and within our city . . . .
- The teachers in our local schools, colleges and universities that . . . .
- Those students that are seeking positions in their chosen fields . . . .

What a joy it is for us to be your servants. Equip and train us in godly living so that by our example and by our words of hope and encouragement, other people's lives will be challenged and brought to a saving knowledge of Jesus Christ. May your Word feed us today. May it energise our will to obey you. This we ask through Jesus Christ our Lord. **AMEN**

Scriptures for private prayer and reflection:

Psalm 16:1-11 : Galatians 5:16-26 : Philippians 4:4

Personal Prayer Topics:

_____

_____

_____

_____

_____

22.

RACIOUS GOD AND FATHER, your mercies are new every morning. There is a wonderful freshness about you as we come into your presence. Each time we come to you it is as if we have never been before. We expect you to surprise us. How we need that freshness and joy that you alone can inspire within us. So often, O Lord, we feel compelled to preserve what we know from the past and as a result of this, so often our faith is backward looking rather than forward reaching. In this way we sadly find our security in what we know rather than in you. Your Word tells us, "not to dwell on the past" because you want to lead us forwards in the adventure of faith. Lord, we know that there are many good things that you have given to us and done for us in the past, and we don't want to minimise them. But, Father, what you have for us today and what you will unfold for us tomorrow requires that we trust you implicitly. You are such a wonderful Lord! You are constantly doing new things! Your creativity and wisdom leave us almost breathless. We come before you today in awe and wonder. Our hearts overflow in praise and worship.

Let us have a time for silent praise and prayer:

Father, we confess that it's not only the good things that we hold on to, but we also cling to those things that we should leave behind us. So often we hold on to our sins and failures when we should relinquish them into your hands seeking your forgiveness so that they will be lost in the sea of your forgetfulness. Enable us, Lord, to do this today. Forgive us Father, for our coldness of heart. Sometimes we become hardened by our constant exposure to the needs of others. Keep us always sensitive to the pain of others. Father, when we have disappointed you; when we have robbed you of your glory; when we have disobeyed your will; when we have ignored the promptings of your Spirit, we pray that you will forgive us. Gracious God, we pray that you will make us holy by the power of your indwelling Spirit. Grant to us a ready obedience to your Word. Amidst all the battles and temptations of life keep us faithful to you and may your joy overflow from our lives bringing hope and confidence and faith into the lives of others.

You have given to us the responsibility to pray for your world and we want to take that challenge seriously this morning.

Gracious God we pray for . . . . (Expand these topics)

- Judges and magistrates that they may not be deceived by clever words; that they may be given wisdom and courage to act justly . . . .
- Christian writers and broadcasters, directors and actors . . . .
- Spiritual renewal in our land . . . .
- The different activities of our church life . . . . (Name some and their needs)
- Students studying in our Bible Colleges and Seminaries . . . .
- The other churches in our city . . . .
- Christians that we know who have lapsed from the Faith . . . .

Grant today, O Lord, that what we have said with our lips, we may believe in our hearts and daily practice in our lives. This we ask through Jesus Christ our Lord. **AMEN**

Scriptures for private prayer and reflection:

Jeremiah 2:1-37 : 1 Corinthians 12 : Hebrews 10:1-18

Personal Prayer Topics:

_____

_____

_____

_____

_____

_____

_____

23.

OUR GRACIOUS GOD AND Father, in the midst of our changing world, what a comfort it is to know that you remain the same - unchanging in all your ways. We never need to be anxious about whether you will receive us when we come to you. We approach you this morning on the basis of your promises to us - that we should come boldly into your presence and that we should present to you the concerns of our hearts. We come, O Lord, because we want to worship you, to reaffirm our faith and trust in you. We come because we need you, because we need to grow in grace and in our knowledge of you.

Gracious Father, we offer our thanks to you for all your many mercies towards us. You have watched over us; you have ministered to our deepest needs; you have revealed yourself to us in the most unexpected circumstances. We thank you, Lord, that when we've been beaten down by depression, when we've been isolated by our despair, that we have been reminded that you are our God and that you will never let us go. You have given us courage and strength to go on. How we thank you for that this morning. May our lives be a continual thank offering to you.

Let's have a time of silence for personal prayers of thanksgiving:

Lord God, as we come before you, we sense the difference between us. You are holy, we are sinful. You are strong and we are weak. In you all the treasures of wisdom and knowledge combine, and by comparison, we are ignorant. We thank you that out of your strength and wisdom you minister to us and that you allow us to draw upon these resources. Forgive us Father, that we are so slow to learn, that we have to repeat so many of the lessons of life. Forgive us Lord that we turn away from you so frequently, when we should really draw nearer to you. So often, O Lord, we prefer to try our own ways first, rather than coming to you. Forgive us, Father, for our sinfulness. So many times we have strayed from you. We fail to respond to the promptings of your Spirit. We ignore what you have told us in your Word. Lord, we bring our brokenness to you this morning, knowing that you will forgive and restore us, so that your glory may rest upon us. Thank you, Lord, for the new hope that you give to us and for the opportunity to begin again under your Lordship.

Lord God, we pray this morning for . . . . (Expand these topics)

- Those who are hurting deep within themselves . . . .
- Those who find all the joy is drained out of their lives . . . .
- Those who find themselves bound by . . . . and desire to be free
- Those who are searching for truth and reality . . . .
- Those whose lives have been touched by sorrow and loss . . . .
- Those who live in the trouble zones of . . . . (Troubled countries of the world)
- Your Church throughout the world that . . . .

O Lord our God, meet with us we pray this morning. May the breath of your Spirit put new life into us, giving us that readiness and willingness to do whatever you ask us to do. May we not put off until tomorrow, what we should really do today. Open within us we pray, the floodgates of love, that we may love you with all our heart, mind and strength and the people around us as ourselves. Minister to us from your Word we pray. Hear the prayer of our hearts as we offer it to you in the wonderful name of our Lord Jesus Christ. **AMEN**

Scriptures for private prayer and reflection:

Matthew 15:1-20 : John 8:1-11 : 2 Corinthians 5:11-21

Personal Prayer Topics:

_____

_____

_____

_____

_____

_____

_____

_____

24.

*U*NIMAGINABLE JOY IS OURS today as we come before you in prayer and worship. As we have walked in faith with you, we have proved the reliability of your Word and your faithfulness. We just thank you that your promises to your people are not a disappointment. Gracious God, we don't find it easy to express our deepest thoughts to you. Words seem such an inadequate instrument with which to praise you. We are so grateful today that you not only hear our words but you can also read our hearts. We just adore you, for you have made us your own. You have brought us into your family. You have endowed us with the riches of heaven. Like the Psalmist of old, we say, "Bless the Lord, O my soul, and all that is within me bless His holy name".

Let us have a time of silent prayer and reflection on the holiness of God:

Your Word encourages us to "worship the Lord in the beauty of holiness". Yet there is something about holiness that makes us feel very uncomfortable. We sense in a new way the depth of our sin and the need of your forgiveness. Sin is merely a word until we come into your holy presence. Then we see it in a completely different light. We see the ugliness of it all. The heartbreak that it brings to you; the destructiveness that it generates in our own lives and the lives of others. Lord, we ask for your forgiveness and the strengthening of our wills to walk in your ways.

As a fellowship of your people we rejoice together and are glad that you are our God and that we are your people. Your gracious dealings with us have put music into our hearts. The melody gets louder as we consider that you are the King of Kings and Lord of Lords. You are the Alpha and the Omega, the beginning and the end of all things. We thank you this morning for the assurance that 'our God reigns', that nothing can dethrone the Creator, or defeat His eternal purposes. We thank you that you have brought us from defeat to ultimate victory through our Lord Jesus Christ. Mighty God, we worship and adore you. Holy is your name. Father we come to you now on behalf of others who need the enabling touch of your grace and the enlivening of your Spirit.

Our Father we pray for . . . . (Expand these topics)

- Those who have lost all purpose for living . . . .
- Those who are unemployed and have been unable to find satisfactory employment . . .
- Those who have lost their homes . . . .
- The pastors of all the local churches . . .
- The street people and those who are homeless – and those who work with them . . . .
- Those in the "sunset years" of their lives . . . .
- Guidance to be given to those who are in government – national, local, state / provincial
- The Church's task of mission throughout the world – (Name any individual missionaries)

Gracious God, we are here this morning because we want you to impact our lives with your truth and to transform us in such a way that the world will recognize that we have been with Jesus. So Father, unstop our ears that we may hear your voice; open our eyes that we may catch a glimpse of your glory; energize our wills that we may leave here determined to obey your mandate with your assistance and strength. As the Psalmist said, "May your word be a lamp to our feet and a light to our path". These things we ask for the glory and honour of your name, through Jesus Christ our Lord. **AMEN**

Scriptures for private reflection and prayer:

Exodus 3:1–6 : Psalm 81:1–16 : Isaiah 6:1–13
1 Corinthians 14:26–33

Personal Prayer Topics:

_____

_____

_____

_____

_____

_____

_____

25.

LMIGHTY GOD, WE COME into your presence this morning with grateful hearts and praise upon our lips. The fact that you have kept your hand on our lives throughout this week has given us confidence and strength. We come to express our thanks and to praise the name of Jesus. There is so much around us to discourage, but your joy has been our strength. Your love has motivated us to serve. Your Holy Spirit has opened our eyes to see new truth as it is revealed in your Word.

Sometimes, Lord, we are slow to respond to your prompting. As a consequence, sometimes opportunities are lost. Forgive us, we pray. Forgive us, Lord, when our love for you grows cold. Sometimes, O Lord, we find ourselves so caught up in the rush and tear of life, that we don't pause long enough to listen to what you are saying. Slow us down we pray, that we may be able to refocus our lives and achieve the purposes you have set before us. Be present among us today. Deepen our relationship with yourself and draw us into a more wholehearted obedience to your Word. This we ask in the name of Jesus Christ our Lord. **AMEN.**

Let us pray for . . . . (Expand these topics)

- Those who have to make life changing decisions . . .
- Christians who live in hostile environments . . . .
- Those serving as missionaries throughout the world . . .
- Christians, who work in the media, enable them to . . .
- Those who wrestle with sleepless nights . . .
- Our military that are facing danger every day . . . .
- Those who are in constant pain and are at their wits end . . . .

The storms of life are no respecter of persons. We pray for the grace and strength to walk on the troubled waters rather than be engulfed or intimidated by them. Tune our ears to listen for your voice. Enliven our faith to respond to your call. Give us the courage to go forward even when everything seems to tell us to stay put. We thank you that nothing in our lives escapes your notice or is beyond the reach of your grace and love. So minister to us this morning from your Word. Enlarge the territory of our ministry and keep your hand continually upon us. We ask this in Jesus' name. **AMEN.**

Scriptures for private reflection and prayer:

John 16:16–33 : 2 Corinthians 6:14–18 : Ephesians 2:11–22

Personal Prayer Topics:

_____

_____

_____

_____

_____

_____

_____

26.

SOVEREIGN LORD, AS WE come into your presence this morning, we would echo the words of the hymn writer and say . . . .

> *All things praise Thee: gracious Lord,*
> *Great Creator, powerful Word.*
> *Omnipresent Spirit, now*
> *At Thy feet we humbly bow.*
> *Lift our hearts in praise to Thee;*
> *All things praise Thee: Lord may we.* (G.W. Conder)

Your love has touched our lives and drawn us closer to you. Your Spirit has opened our eyes to see your glory. You have changed our deafness into hearing so that your Word may take root in our hearts. You have lifted us out of our sin and shame and granted us forgiveness through the death of Jesus on the cross. This morning we worship and adore you as a company of your redeemed people. So, Lord God, minister to each of us today according to what we need rather than what we want, so that our lives may more clearly bear the stamp of Christ upon them. This we ask in His holy name. **AMEN**

Let us have a few moments of silent prayer and reflection:

Let us pray for . . . . (Expand these topics)

- World governments as they seek to battle terrorism . . .
- Christians that they may not be paralyzed by fear . . . .
- Those in our fellowship who are sick . . . (Name with their permission)
- Our church organizations . . . . (Naming them & their needs)
- Our church leaders . . . . (Elders, Deacons, etc.)
- The persecuted Church around the world . . . .

Even though it appears that evil has the upper hand in our world, we pray that it may be overcome by the power of your love and goodness, directed by your Spirit. Your Word assures us that the ultimate victory is yours, that Satan is a defeated enemy. May this truth uphold us in difficult times. Turn the hearts of those who would destroy, to constructive and creative endeavours. Help us to be faithful in prayer. Help us to reach out to those around us, enabling them to accept your hope, to replace the sense of hopelessness that often overshadows their lives. May we be better able to share with confidence our faith in you, with those who are struggling to make sense of their lives. Touch our lives by your mighty power we pray, through Jesus Christ our Lord. **AMEN**

Scriptures for private reflection and prayer:

Matthew 23:1-39 : Matthew 25:31-46 : Mark 8:1-13

Personal Prayer Topics:

_____

_____

_____

_____

_____

_____

_____

_____

27.

GRACIOUS GOD AND FATHER, we join our voices in praise of your holy name. As we declare your mighty acts, we rejoice in your faithfulness. As we look at your creation, we marvel at its detail and intricacies. We thank you for the gift of your Word, which speaks life to our souls. We thank you for the wonder of your forgiveness, which brings us into the freedom of your Spirit and empowers us for your service. We thank you for sending Christ into the world to be our Saviour and Lord. Guide us, we pray, in our worship today. Make us aware of your holy presence. Lord, at times we display hardheartedness to others, and we allow others to unnecessarily bear our burdens. Sometimes our words do not reflect what is going on in our minds and hearts. Cleanse us from our sins that mar our Christian witness and alienate others from coming to you for forgiveness and life. Strengthen us where we are weak, and draw us into closer fellowship with you. Impart your Spirit to us, so that we may be better equipped to serve you. We ask this for your name's sake. **AMEN**

Let's have a time of silent prayer when we can open our hearts to God and seek His grace to help in time of need:

Let us remember in our prayers today . . . . (Expand these topics)

- The leaders of our country . . . .
- The situation in the Middle East . . . . The Word of God as it goes out over radio and TV today . . . .
- The ministry of . . . . (Name some Christian organizations)
- The unemployed in our fellowship . . . .

Gracious God, grant us the ability to listen to what you are saying to us. As we listen, help us to understand and do what you are asking of us. We cannot manipulate you or bargain with you. You are God. We pray that you will be the forgiver and leader of our lives. Minister to us through your Word today. May the power of your saving grace reach into the darkest corners of our lives, renewing us, changing us, and equipping us for the living of these days. These things we ask in the name of Jesus Christ our forgiver and Lord. **AMEN**

Scriptures for private reflection and prayer:

1 Kings 3:1-28 : Psalm 119:97-98 : Ecclesiastes 8:1-8 : James 1:5

Personal Prayer Topics:

_____

_____

_____

_____

_____

_____

_____

28.

AS WE COME INTO your presence this morning, we do so with praise and thanksgiving. Apart from your faithfulness and your mercy we would not be here. You have provided for us in every way. You have been with us every day this week. You have worked all things together for good, even those things we have disliked. We thank you this morning that you are for us and not against us.

Forgive us, Lord, for those times we have insisted on our own way rather than going yours. Forgive us when we may have hurt others. Forgive us when the "busyness" of life has made us forget all about you. We are so grateful that you did not forget about us. We ask today that you will remove any barrier in our hearts that would prevent us from responding to the voice of your Spirit. Meet with us we pray during this service of worship. Strengthen us. Challenge us. Humble us so that we may be more able to be your representatives in the world around us.

Where there is hurt, may we bring healing; where there is strife, may we bring your peace; where there is confusion, may we bring a glimpse of your direction and be able to point people to Jesus.

Make us channels of your blessings to others. So Lord, accept the worship of our hearts as we present our praise and petitions to you this morning in the name of our Lord and Saviour Jesus Christ. **AMEN**

Let us have a time of quiet reflection and prayer:

Let us pray for . . . . (Expand these topics)

- Those in our fellowship in special need . . . .
- Our young people as they seek to find their calling in life . . . .
- Our senior citizens with their specific needs . . . .
- The continent of Africa that is ravaged by HIV and AIDS . . . .
- Those who translate the Bible into different languages . . . .
- Those who are struggling to handle the changes in their lives . . . .

Gracious God, one of the things all of us find difficult to handle is change. Yet you are the God who continually makes all things new. Change is an integral part of your creative work within us. So equip us by your Spirit to be able to handle the changes that confront us so that we might turn them into blessings. We pray that your Word may take root in our hearts and bear fruit for your Kingdom. We thank you Lord that our lives are in a constant state of redevelopment. You are changing us more and more into the image of the Lord Jesus Christ. Continue this work we pray, so that others might be helped by our witness and encouraged by our work. This we ask for your glory's sake through Christ our Lord. **AMEN**

Scriptures for private reflection and prayer:

Deuteronomy 29:1-29 : Mark 4:35-41 : 2 Corinthians 5:11-21
Hebrews 13:1-25

Personal Prayer Topics:

_____

_____

_____

_____

_____

_____

_____

_____

29.

WE ENTER YOUR PRESENCE this morning with praise on our lips and thankfulness in our hearts. Throughout another week we have proved your faithfulness. As we have relied on your strength, you have supported us. As we have touched the lives of others, your love has filled our hearts and overflowed to them. As we have stood for that which is right, you have given us courage. So this morning we magnify your holy name. How great you are!

Your Word tells us - "That God is light and in Him is no darkness at all". When we look into our own hearts, we see those areas where the light of your presence has not yet shined. We pray, shine into our hearts today. Dispel the gloom and darkness, so that we might walk in closer fellowship with you. In your mercy forgive us when we have responded to the lure of sin rather than to the voice of your Spirit. Heal our brokenness we pray, that we might more readily be the light of the world around us, which you have called us to be.

Release us from those things that would hamper our worship today. Free us from those restraints that form a barrier to the working of your Spirit. Deliver us from publicly standing up for principles that we do not practice in private. Create in us, O Lord, a clean heart and renew a right spirit within us. Put music into our hearts and a song of praise on our lips. May your Word bring forth fruit in our lives for your glory. This we ask through Jesus Christ our Lord. **AMEN**

Let us have a time of silence – The Bible says, "Be still and know that I am God; I will be exalted among the nations, I will be exalted in the earth". (Psalm 46:10)

Let us pray for . . . . (Expand these topics)

- Those who work overseas in education, medicine, business and missions . . . .
- Those in our community grieving the loss of loved ones . . . .
- New immigrants as they seek to settle into our country and community . . . .
- Your Church in our country to be revived by the Spirit of God . . .
- Those who work in the media that they may focus on truth . . . .

Gracious God, we would pray for ourselves. Enable us by your Spirit to share our faith more effectively and with a greater sensitivity. Empower us to reach out around us to those who are hurting so that we may be able to bring hope and healing to them. Deepen our love for you. After our worshipping here today, may you be able to express yourself more clearly and effectively through us. This we ask through Jesus Christ our Lord and Saviour. **AMEN**

An offering prayer:

We have received new life through your generosity, O Lord. Christ has given us hope in the midst of despair. Enable us to make our offering this morning with thanksgiving and praise, so that we may be known as God's generous people. We ask this for the glory of your name and the building up of your Church. **AMEN**

Scriptures for private reflection and prayer:

Matthew 5:13-16 : John 1:4-5 : James 1:22-25

Personal Prayer Topics:

_____

_____

_____

_____

_____

_____

_____

30.

RACIOUS GOD, WE THANK you that we can gather in this way this morning. We have come to meet with you and express our thanks and praise. We so appreciate all the many blessings you bestow on us. Your generosity is beyond measure. We thank you that you sent Christ into the world so that we might come to know you and experience new life through faith in Him and experience the wonder of your forgiveness. We thank you for the gift of the Bible that guides and inspires us as your Holy Spirit interprets it to our hearts and minds. May this time that we spend with you be truly profitable. Challenge us. Rebuke us. Inspire us. Change us. Open our eyes to see you as you really are. Help us not to stereotype you. Speak to us in a way that we can understand and to which we can respond. So hear the prayer of our hearts as we offer it to you.

Let us express to God in silent prayer the deep concerns of our hearts:

Father we are aware of the deceitfulness of our own hearts. We can speak thoughtlessly. We can pry into things where we should never go. We often conceal the real motives for doing things and appear to others better than we are. How many times O Lord we deceive ourselves as to where our true duty lies. Father, forgive us and by the power of your Spirit renew us and put us back on the road of righteousness. Restore to us the joy of our salvation. Thank you Lord for all that you have done for us. May our lives reflect the changes you have made within us. To your name be all the glory and praise through Jesus Christ our Lord. **AMEN**

Let us pray for . . . . (Expand these topics)

- Doctors, nurses and all engaged in the ministry of healing . . . .
- Peace in the Middle East . . . .
- Those who mourn . . . .
- Those engaged in preaching the gospel around the world . . . .
- Those engaged in the relief of poverty and hunger . . . .
- All high school teachers and administrators . . . .
- Those who work in the "helping agencies" around the world . . . .

Gracious God, as we look around your world and in particular where your Kingdom is truly manifested we see wonderful things taking place. Where the powers of darkness and evil hold sway, we see death and destruction. How we long for that day when "the earth shall be filled with the knowledge of God as the waters cover the sea". May our citizenship in your Kingdom enable us to make a difference in the world we see around us. So equip us by your Spirit, that we might be truly your ambassadors. So Lord God, glorify yourself through your Church. Make us living examples of your love and grace. May our words give direction and help. May our actions lift people up and inspire hope. Like the disciples of old, we say, 'Lord, teach us to pray'. May our homes be outposts of your Kingdom, where others might find peace and refreshment and discover your salvation in Jesus Christ. So minister to us now, by your Spirit, for we ask this in the name of Jesus Christ our Lord. **AMEN**

Scriptures for private reflection and prayer:

Psalm 46:1-11 : Galatians 6:1-10 : Colossians 2:13-15
Hebrews 4:15-16

Personal Prayer Topics:

_____

_____

_____

_____

_____

_____

_____

31.

GRACIOUS GOD AND FATHER, we never cease to marvel at your great wisdom and power. Your wisdom is unconventional. Your power is absolute. You truly rule the universe that you have created. We praise and magnify your name today. You are the great architect of the Church and we thank you for making us part of it through the death of Christ on the cross and through His glorious resurrection. We give you thanks for the forgiveness you have freely bestowed on us and your gift of eternal life.

We pray that you will lift from our hearts any restrictions that we have laid on ourselves that might hinder our worship today. We have come together to meet with you; to fellowship with you; to receive your word to us. Pour out your Spirit upon us O Lord that we might see your glory and hear your voice deep within our hearts and give glory, honour and praise to you.

Lord, we don't always find it easy to recognize your presence. Often our spirits are downcast and disappointment clouds our vision. Open our eyes this morning to the undiscovered secrets of your Word. Set our hearts on fire with your love and send us on our way rejoicing. Help us never to forget your mercy and your grace and the presence of your indwelling Spirit in our lives.

Forgive us, O Lord, for the doubting and suspicion with which we sometimes regard you. Grant us more faith as we commit to obeying your Word. We so often have faith in those whom we do not know, and yet we are reluctant to focus all our faith in you. Minister to us from your Word today. Enable us to take hold of eternal things. Develop within us your divine perspective on life. Fill us with your Spirit. We ask this in the name of our risen and reigning Lord. **AMEN**

Introduce a time of silent prayer with: We cannot see His form, but we can feel His presence. He knows all about us. He waits by appointment to speak to us reassurance, comfort and forgiveness. Let us, in silence, tell Him of our needs in our own words and to open our hearts and minds to receive from Him what He wants to give to us.

Pause for a short period:

Gracious God, as you read our heart's desires, we pray that you will meet our deepest needs. Transform us by your grace through Jesus Christ our Lord. **AMEN**

Let us pray for . . . . (Expand these topics)

- All those who are retired, that they may see new opportunities of service to use the gifts God has given them . . . .
- All missionaries who serve in dangerous places . . . .
- Those who are suffering because of natural disasters . . . .
- Our nation that it may be a blessing and not a curse to other nations . . . .
- Nations to exercise greater stewardship of the environment . . . .

Gracious God, it's so easy for us to become comfortable as we live in a world that is in rebellion against you. There are so many people who are lost that need to be found by the Lord Jesus Christ. Awaken us to the opportunities that are around us for touching the lives of others with the grace and power of God. Put a new song within our hearts. Give us the Good News to speak that will challenge, encourage, and bless others. May Christ be seen in us and be able to minister through us. This we ask for His name's sake. **AMEN**

Scriptures for private reflection and prayer:

Luke 12:1-12 : 2 Corinthians 1:3-11 : Galatians 6:2

Personal Prayer Topics:

_____

_____

_____

_____

_____

_____

_____

_____

32.

GRACIOUS GOD AND FATHER, we thank you this morning that you have revealed yourself to us. We know who you are and what you have done for us through the Lord Jesus Christ. We praise you that you have brought us into your family. We thank you that you have imparted to us your Holy Spirit that we might be able to effectively live, serve and worship you. We thank you that you are always available to us and are unchanging in your dealings with us. Daily we rely on your strength and power to equip us and sustain us.

Forgive us, Lord, when we become forgetful of your presence with us and act on our own understanding without any reference to you. Forgive us when we have allowed resentment and bitterness to colour our relationships. Lord Jesus, we thank you for paying the price for our forgiveness and giving to us your great gift of eternal life and reconciliation to God.

Draw us closer to yourself this morning as we worship you. Open our eyes to see your glory. May the voice of your Spirit, speak clearly to us deep in our hearts. O Lord, we offer you our worship and praise, and we do so in the name of Jesus Christ our Lord. **AMEN**

Let us have a time of silent prayer and reflection:

In these few moments help us to remember what you have impressed upon our hearts and minds. Enable us to follow through in obedience so that your will can be achieved. May your Word always be the incentive for our service. This we ask for your name's sake. **AMEN**

Let us pray for . . . . (Expand these topics)

- Those imprisoned for their faith in Christ Jesus . . .
- Those who feel there is no purpose left for living . . . .
- All Church leaders around the world . . . .
- Young people in our country to have openness to the Gospel . . . .
- Those areas where there is famine, hunger and disease . . . .

O Lord our God, as we pause before you during this time of worship, we acknowledge that we don't always find it easy to pray. So often we become preoccupied with our own inner struggles with sin. The things that are waiting to be done suddenly come back to mind and cause us to rush our communion with you. Lord, we find it so hard to focus our thoughts on you because of the Enemy's distractions that begin to assail our minds, when we are quiet before you. Lord Jesus, we are confident this morning that you understand us. You have walked this earth as a man. You have felt the pull of temptation. You have felt the pressure of the "busyness" of the world around. Lord, be the focal point of our worship today. Enable us by the power of your Spirit, to rise above the things that would distract us. Fire our hearts with new devotion. Release within us your love that we might be caught up in heart to heart fellowship with you. Free us from the chain of distractions.

We thank you for your patience with us. You never give up on us. You constantly nudge us by your Spirit, so that we might walk in your ways. We thank you for the gift of life and for extending to us your forgiveness. We thank you for your church and the mutual strengthening that is gained by being part of it.

Gracious God, we know how much we need the ministry of your Spirit within our hearts. Forgive our sins and failures. Heal our hurts and bring wholeness to our brokenness. As we open our lives to you now, renew us by your grace. May your Word take root within our hearts and continually direct our lives. This we ask through Jesus Christ our Lord. **AMEN**

Scriptures for private prayer and reflection:

Psalm 146:1-10 : Psalm 92:1-15 : Romans 2:1-16
Ephesians 1:7-8

Personal Prayer Topics:

33.

OUR GRACIOUS GOD, AS we gather in your house this morning, for some of us, memories will burn their way into consciousness. They will bring to the fore unrealized dreams and maybe a sense of loss. We thank you that in our suffering world, you suffer with us, so grant us your strength to go on and give us your peace to garrison our hearts and minds. We recognize O Lord that the strife we see in the world around us is but a reflection of the warring desires within the human heart. Gracious God, we pray for a change of heart in our world and also in us, for there is no other way for life to be transformed. Minister today to those whose memories are painful. Be very real to those who have loved ones living and working in areas where there is terrorist activity and persecution of your Church.

Gracious God, inspire our worship today by your Spirit. By your grace lift us up to that place where we can worship you in spirit and in truth. Take from our lives the strain and stress and let our ordered lives confess the beauty of your peace.

Father, how we long to be more like Jesus. Yet we find our lives tarnished by the influences of the world around us. Like the Psalmist of old, our sin seems to be ever before us. So we come this morning seeking your forgiveness for those things that have created a barrier between us, and have built walls between us and those around us. Renew us in mind and spirit we pray. Strengthen us where we are weak. Replace any sense of despair with your gift of hope. Where we are hurting, impart your healing. Gracious God, perform your surgery on our souls this morning as we study your Word together. We ask this in Jesus' name. **AMEN.**

Let us have a few moments of silent prayer and reflection, asking God to focus our attention on Him, so that we may be responsive to the leading of His Spirit:

Thank you, Lord, for hearing our prayer and ministering to us. Fill our lives with your Spirit so that Jesus might be seen and heard through us. To your name be praise and glory. **AMEN**

Let's pray for . . . . (Expand these topics)

- The nations around the globe that are divided, broken and war torn . . . .
- The witness of the local churches in high risk areas . . . .
- Those who serve as missionaries around the world . . . .
- The leaders of our nation to act with integrity and pursue righteousness . . . .
- Those in special need in our fellowship . . . .

Your Word teaches us O Lord, that the better we know you, the more able we are to serve you. Deepen our relationship with you. Wherever we go may we be agents of reconciliation, bringing people closer to each other and closer to you. As the strains and stresses of life seek to bend and break us, may we turn to you for new strength. Make us equal to the challenges around us and within us. Gracious God, grant us your forgiveness for those things that have marred our relationship with you, and strained our relationships with others. Renew a right spirit in us, we pray. This we ask in the name of Jesus Christ our Lord and Saviour. **AMEN**

Scriptures for private prayer and reflection:

Matthew 16:21-28 : Luke 21:17-19 : John 9:2-3
1 Thessalonians 3:1-8 : Hebrews 2:18 : James 1:2-8

Personal Prayer Topics:

_____

_____

_____

_____

_____

_____

_____

34.

GRACIOUS GOD AND FATHER, we bring our praise and adoration to you. You have made us alive with your life. You have awakened us to the glory of another day and summoned us to worship, that we might experience a fresh outpouring of your love and grace. We affirm today that you are our Father and we are your people. We thank you for the gift of your Son the Lord Jesus Christ to be our Saviour. During this short time of worship, direct and control our thoughts that we may focus wholly upon you. Grant us reverence as we remember your glory, and penitence as we focus on your holiness. Enable us to be grateful in the light of your love, so that when we leave this service this morning, we may do so with a deeper knowledge of you; with our love for you and others rekindled, and having experienced a renewing touch of your Holy Spirit to strengthen and equip us for the days ahead.

Gracious God, we are still in the process of growing as your people. We err in our actions. We utter words that hurt and damage relationships. We seek after those things that are not on your list of priorities for us. Sometimes we shut our eyes to the opportunities that you set before us to be your ambassadors. So Lord, we seek your forgiveness as we bow in your presence.

Throughout this day, O Lord, let us touch the lives of others for good, by the power of your Spirit, whether it is through the words we speak or the prayers we breathe or the lives we live, or the things we do. These things we ask in the wonderful name of Jesus Christ our Lord. **AMEN**

In the quietness of our own hearts, let us give thanks to God for all His love and patience towards us:

Let us pray for . . . . (Expand these topics)

- Those who feel overwhelmed by their difficulties . . . .
- The homeless people in our city . . . .
- Those who serve in local and national government . . . .
- The professors and teachers in our colleges and universities . . . .
- Students who are trying to maintain a Christian witness in colleges . . . .
- A spiritual awakening in our community . . . .

Gracious God, if we are going to do your work, we need a fresh filling of your Spirit daily to equip us and direct us. Refresh us by your presence. May your Word increasingly become for us a treasure trove of truth. May we be a light in the darkness of the world around us, leading people to you who are the Light of the World. Deepen our concern for those who do not know you. Minister to us to that end, because we ask it in the name of Jesus Christ our Lord. **AMEN**

Scriptures for private prayer and reflection:

Matthew 10:19-20 : John 3:5-7, 4:23-24, 14:15-31 : Acts 1:8
2 Corinthians 12:9-10 : Ephesians 3:16, 18-19

Personal Prayer Topics:

_____

_____

_____

_____

_____

_____

_____

35.

RACIOUS GOD, WE JOIN together in praise this morning for the generous way in which you have bestowed your blessings on us. But we have to confess, sometimes we are more grateful for the gifts bestowed on us, than for the Giver Himself. How we thank you this morning that you have not abandoned your world to chaos and confusion, but that you still hold the world in your hands. You still direct the paths of your people. You still confront evil. You are still Sovereign over the history of this world. Sometimes we forget that you are the Creator, omnipotent God. All heaven worships you and so do we this morning.

We confess that sometimes when a great deliverance has come our way - like a return to health, or a financial bonus, or reconciliation with a friend - that we are truly grateful. But so often as time passes and the crisis is over we return to our old ways and show little concern for your will in our lives. Lord, we ask you to forgive us. You have said in your word, that "if we confess our sins, God is faithful and just and will forgive us our sins and cleanse us from all unrighteousness". So Father, we claim that promise this morning.

Please remove any barriers that would prevent us from worshipping you today. Pour out your Spirit on us. Open our eyes to see your matchless splendor, so that we may respond to your voice. This we ask through Jesus Christ our Saviour. **AMEN**

Let us pause for a moment of silent prayer, as we bring to God our personal concerns:

Lord you have told us to seek you, to ask and to knock. This we have done. So Father we are expecting to find what we are looking for, to receive what we have asked for, and for those doors to be opened that have seemed closed. For we ask this in Jesus' name. **AMEN**

Let us pray for . . . . (Expand these topics)

- Fellow Christians who are persecuted. More than 40 countries persecute Christians . . . .
- Israel and the Palestinian problem . . . .
- Wisdom in the development of urban ministries . . . .
- Those who serve in the military . . . .
- Safety from terrorist activity on world airlines . . . .

Gracious and Eternal God, as we have brought the needs of others to you, our own needs are never far from our minds. You know those things that perplex us and sometimes cause us to stumble. We would pray for our families - those who love you and serve you, that you would guide and encourage them, that their lives may bring glory to you. We think of those whose love for you has grown cold; who no longer worship you; who make numerous excuses to avoid meeting with you. Speak to their hearts and minds, we pray. Lead them back to yourself. Defeat the Enemy's efforts to lead them away from you into a lost eternity.

Lord God, we need your refreshing touch on our own lives this morning, to invigorate our faith, deepen our devotion and consecrate our service. May the truth of your Word challenge us and the working of your Spirit convict us, so that we may grow in grace and in our knowledge of you. May all that we have read in your Word be translated into action during this coming week, so that others might see our good works and glorify you, our heavenly Father. This we ask through Jesus Christ our Lord. **AMEN**

Scriptures for private prayer and reflection:

Exodus 10:2 : Deuteronomy 6:6-7 : Matthew 5:11-12
Ephesians 3:14-15

Personal Prayer Topics:

_____

_____

_____

_____

_____

_____

_____

36.

WE HAVE COME TOGETHER this morning to worship and praise your holy name. We have come to meet with you and to listen to your Word and how we should apply it to our lives. We have come so that you may continue your work of reshaping our lives, so that they may conform more readily to that of our Lord Jesus Christ. We thank you for your invitation to come and worship. We thank you that you have brought us into the family of God. We pray that as we rub shoulders with one another and share the way you have been with us, and the strength and guidance you have given us, that it will sharpen our witness and deepen our commitment to you. May our lives be a continual challenge and encouragement to others.

Forgive us, Lord, for those things that have marred our lives and interrupted our communication with you. Forgive us when we have done our own thing rather than walk in your way. We thank you that the penalty for our sin was paid at the cross by the Lord Jesus. Your Word reminds us, that "without the shedding of blood there is no remission of sin". So we rejoice this morning in the knowledge that there is now no condemnation for those who are in Christ Jesus. Draw us closer to yourself today. Pour your Spirit upon us. Stir the depths of our hearts with new love for you. May your presence be real to us today and may we be strengthened by it.

Let us have a time of silent prayer and reflection:

Thank you Lord, for hearing our prayer and touching our lives with your grace and power. We praise and magnify your name, through Jesus Christ our Lord. **AMEN**

Let us pray for . . . . (Expand these topics)

- The other churches in our community . . . . (Name them)
- The agencies that minister to the poor and underprivileged in our city . . . .
- The Christians who face persecution in Islamic countries . . . .
- Those who minister to patients in nursing homes . . . .
- Hospital and military chaplains . . . .
- Mayors and city councilors that they may seek the good of the community . . .

Lord God, you have a passion for people. Instill that same passion into our hearts. Help us to recognize needs even when they are not apparent, and to minister to them in your name. There are so many around us who do not know you, and who live lives that are lost. Help us to build bridges to them over which they may travel to find you. Impact their lives for eternity, O Lord. May we respond to your Word to us today, for we ask it in Jesus' name. **AMEN**

Scriptures for private prayer and reflection:

Exodus 3:1-6 : Psalm 81:1-16 : John 4:23-24
1 Corinthians 14:26

Personal Prayer Topics:

_____

_____

_____

_____

_____

_____

37.

WE THANK YOU, O Lord our God, for the precious gift of this day. A day in which we can come together to praise and magnify your holy name. With deep gratitude we acknowledge your steadfast love towards us. We thank you for the assurance of your presence with us. You have said, "I am with you always, to the end of the age". In the midst of the chaos of our modern world, we pause to acknowledge that all authority and power are yours. No events in this world take you by surprise. We thank you that nothing can separate us from your love - whether it is life or death, events of today or tomorrow, or anything else in the whole world. You support us every day with the power of your Spirit.

Yet, O Lord, we recognize that our lives are stained by sin. At times we ignore your presence. We allow anxiety to rule our lives and dictate our actions. We fail to witness when the opportunity is given to us. We keep silent when we should speak. At times we have entertained wrong attitudes; we have been more concerned about ourselves than we have about your Kingdom. Often we equate respectability with holiness. Father, we pray that you will forgive us and restore to us the joy of your salvation and set our feet firmly on the road of righteousness.

Our Father, we pray that you will accept our worship and thanksgiving. Draw near to us and minister to us. Where we are weak, make us strong. Where we are blind, enable us to see. Where we are deaf, help us to hear what you are saying to us, so that we may be more Christ-like in all we are and do. We ask this for the glory of your name, through Jesus Christ our Lord. **AMEN**

Let us have a time of silent prayer and reflection:

Thank you for hearing us and showing to us more clearly your will and purpose. **AMEN**

Let us pray for . . . . (Expand these topics)

- Those whose lives are paralyzed by fear and anxiety . . . .
- Those who face constant danger in their employment – police, firemen . . .
- Those involved in Christian broadcasting – script writers, producers, directors, . . .
- The security and border services . . . .
- The mission organizations that we support – (Name them and their needs) . . . .

Gracious God, as we focus on our responsibilities as your people in the areas of our service and in the utilization of our time and giving, we pray that you will open our hearts afresh to your love and grace. Enable us by your Spirit to be found faithful.

Where we are fearful of trusting you, develop our faith. Where we lack courage, empower us by your Spirit. Where we are blind to opportunities, open our eyes to see what you have given to us. So minister to us from your Word today, for we ask it in the name of Jesus Christ our Lord. **AMEN**

Scriptures for private prayer and reflection:

Esther 4:14 : Proverbs 3:5-6 : Matthew 6:25-34 : Luke 14:25-35
James 1:22, 2:14-26

Personal Prayer Topics:

_____

_____

_____

_____

_____

_____

_____

38.

ALMIGHTY GOD, WE JOIN our hearts and voices together this morning in praise and worship. You are our God and you have made us your people. You have granted us forgiveness through our Lord Jesus Christ. You have imparted your Holy Spirit to us. You have refashioned our lives in a dynamic way and so we can truly come before you with gratitude.

Lead us in our thinking as we worship you. Open our hearts that we might be receptive to your grace. May we reciprocate your love. As you have gathered us together, expectation wells up within us. We pray that the purpose for which you brought us here this morning may be fulfilled. Deliver us from the routine that robs us of any sense of reality. Penetrate our lives and reveal to us our needs. Sometimes circumstances overwhelm us and we find it difficult to move forwards in our lives. Lord God, grant us the strength that will make us more than conquerors. May we not leave this place today without having received a word from you.

Let us have a time of silent prayer and reflection:

Lord God, daily as we seek to follow you we constantly struggle with besetting sin. Destructive anger so often wells up within us.

Our actions often betray a lack of trust in you. At times we find it hard to forgive others who have wronged us. Father, this morning as we open our lives before you, we pray for your forgiveness and that you will renew a right spirit within us, so that the likeness of Christ may be more readily visible in our lives. We ask this in Jesus' name. **AMEN**

Let us pray for . . . . (Expand these topics)

- Opportunities to share the Gospel . . . .
- Those in the church fellowship who are unwell (Name them with permission) . . .
- Those who are embittered by the circumstances of their lives . . . .
- Families that are breaking up . . . .
- The ministry of Intervarsity Fellowship . . . .
- Children whose parents are separated . . . .

Almighty God, even though you stretched out the universe in which we live, and you maintain it by your powerful Word, you still have time for each of us. You know us by name and constantly seek to lead us into deeper fellowship with yourself. Minister to us as we lift up the name of Jesus. May we receive of your grace today that our lives may be enriched and our witness sharpened. Enable us to take reproof where it is needed. This we ask through Christ our Lord. **AMEN**

Scriptures for private prayer and reflection:

Proverbs 3:3-7 : Ephesians 3:7-9 : Philippians 1:14
2 Thessalonians 1:1-12

Personal Prayer Topics:

_____

_____

_____

_____

_____

_____

_____

39.

O GOD OUR FATHER, WE adore you and come to lay our lives before you, and to reaffirm our love for you. Your strength has brought us through this past week. Your guidance has led us through the maze of our differing circumstances. Your Word has refreshed us as we have read it day by day. We give you praise, for you have done great things for us and today we are glad.

Thank you, Lord, for your promise to be with us at all times. We know that you have been there. We have felt those gentle nudges in stressful moments. When we have been tempted to feel alone, the warmth of your presence and the promises in your Word, have dispelled our loneliness.

Forgive us, Lord, when we take these things for granted. Forgive us that so often our thanksgiving is confined to words rather than being demonstrated in our living. Deliver us from the seductive influences of sin. Enable us to continue to build positive relationships with those around us. Father, so often we fail you. Opportunities for service are missed. We fail to speak those words of encouragement to those who have lost their zest for living. So often we don't allow you to be "number one" in our lives. Gracious God, grant us your forgiveness, we pray. Strengthen us where we are weak and vulnerable. Help us to keep our eyes firmly fixed on you.

Holy Spirit of God, move among us this morning. Draw us more into line with Christ's purposes. Make us to be true building blocks within your Church. This we ask in Jesus' name. **AMEN**

Let's have a time of silent prayer and reflection:

Father, so often it is when we are quiet that you reveal yourself to us. Thank you for these moments of personal communion with you in Jesus' name. **AMEN**

Let us continue to pray for . . . . (Expand these topics)

- All members of government . . . .
- The turbulent Middle East . . . .
- The hurting people in our community . . . .
- The youth and senior citizens in our community . . . .

May what you have done for us in the past stimulate our faith and trust for the future. Help us to honestly face the issues that confront us. We know O Lord that you will not allow us to face more than we can handle with the strength you give us. May this day be a significant moment in our lives. Pour out your Spirit upon us and open our eyes to see your glory. We ask this in the name of Christ our Lord. **AMEN.**

Scriptures for private prayer and reflection:

Psalm 92:1-15 : Romans 1:18-23 : Matthew 7:7-14
Matthew 23:1-12

Personal Prayer Topics:

_____

_____

_____

_____

_____

_____

_____

_____

40.

O GOD, WITH JOY IN our hearts we come this morning to celebrate in worship; to lift up your holy name, and to express our praise and thanksgiving. For the gift of life and the blessing of salvation, we praise you, O Lord. You have brought us together this morning so that we might give you glory, honour and praise. But you've also brought us into your presence that you might bestow on us your mercy and grace, so that we might reflect in our lives more of you to the world around us. We thirst for you Lord, because you are the "water of life".

Take from our lives O Lord, those things that interrupt our fellowship; that hinder our prayer life and distract us from your Word. Forgive us Father, when we have done those things that have caused you displeasure. Reaffirm for us, that in Christ there is now no condemnation. So may we freely love you and serve you.

In this next hour O Lord, pour out your Holy Spirit upon us. Renew us in our innermost being and change us that Jesus may be more clearly seen in us. As we travel along the road of life, enable us to cast our cares upon you with the full knowledge that you really do care about us, and will provide for us. So lead us through this hour of worship we pray. For Christ's sake we ask it. **AMEN**

Scriptures for private prayer and reflection:

Psalm 16:1-11 : Galatians 5:16-26 : Philippians 4:1-23

Personal Prayer Topics:

_____

_____

_____

_____

_____

_____

_____

_____

41.

GRACIOUS GOD, WE THANK you that in Jesus Christ you have opened the way into your presence. We come before you with praise and thanksgiving. You are a wonderful God. By your grace you have drawn us to yourself. You have taken away our sin. You have supplied our every need and made us equal to all the challenges of life. Praise be to your holy name!

Lord God, we thirst for a deeper relationship with you. Every day sin and self mar the image of Christ that you are developing in us. Forgive us, we pray, for our many failures. Remove the tarnish of the world from our lives, so that your glory may be seen more clearly. So often our lives are filled with regrets. We see the lost opportunities. We see lives that have been embittered by our thoughtless actions. We regret the times that we have been silent when we could have spoken a word of encouragement and hope. Forgive us, Father, for all those things that have marred our witness for you and failed to bring others closer to your Kingdom.

Let's have a time of silent prayer and reflection:

Holy Spirit of God, we welcome you in this place today. Touch our lives with your renewing power. Enliven our faith. Prepare us for the Master's service, so that the lost may be found, the despairing find hope and the bewildered find certainty. This we ask through Jesus who said, "I am the way, the truth and the life. No one comes to the Father but by me". **AMEN**

Let us pray for . . . . (Expand these topics)

- Those who are kept awake by anxiety or suspense . . . .
- Those whose work involves great danger . . .
- The media to focus more on truth and righteousness . . . .
- Spiritual renewal in our land . . . .
- The restless youth in our cities . . .

Thank you Lord for hearing our prayer. We will be looking to see how you answer. In all things may glory come to your name through Jesus Christ our Lord. **AMEN**

Scriptures for private prayer and reflection:

Psalm 146:1-10 : Psalm 103:1-22 : Hebrews 13:1-25

Personal Prayer Topics:

_____

_____

_____

_____

_____

42.

GRACIOUS GOD, WE COME before you this morning with thankfulness and praise. We have received so much from your hand. You have never let us down over the years, even though we have failed you many times. We praise you for your faithfulness. You never change. We thank you for the hope that you have placed within our hearts; a hope that is not mere wishful thinking and does not disappoint, because it is based on the promises of your Word. We praise you for the richness of the inheritance that you have given to us in Jesus Christ. We thank you today for the daily strength and guidance that you give to us, enabling us to do those things that have to be done. Gracious God, we are grateful that you give us the desire and ability to do your will and be a blessing to those around us. As we celebrate your love today, minister to us. May we get to know you better. May we learn to draw more frequently upon your resources. Open our eyes this morning to behold your glory and to receive your Spirit. We ask this through Jesus Christ our Lord. **AMEN**

Let us have a time of silent prayer and reflection:

Lord, we confess that often we have allowed the world to influence our thinking and determine our actions. We have done that which is convenient rather than that which is consistent with life in the Kingdom of God. Forgive us, Father, for the times we have given in to temptation. Your Word teaches us, we shall not be tempted beyond what we can bear, so forgive us that we failed to reach out to you for the grace that you provide that will enable us to stand our ground and gain victory. So now, we humbly reach out to receive your forgiveness. Grant us your enabling grace and power. Give us a clear awareness of the evil around us and of your resources available to us. This we ask through Jesus Christ our Redeemer. **AMEN.**

In preparation for intercession read the following . . . .

James Montgomery wrote: -

> Prayer is the soul's sincere desire
> Uttered or unexpressed.
> The motion of a hidden fire
> That trembles in the breast
>
> O Thou by whom we come to God
> The Life, the Truth, the Way,
> The path of prayer Thyself hast trod,
> Lord, teach us how to pray.

Let us pray for . . . . (Expand these topics)

- The Church in big cities as it seeks to combat the powers of evil . . . .
- All Church leaders that they may be led by God's Spirit . . . .
- The Church in developing countries . . . .
- The Church in areas where terrorism is rife . . . .

Gracious God, tune our minds to be responsive to your truth. Open our hearts to receive your love. Constrain our wills to follow in the paths you indicate to us. Perform your surgery on our souls today we pray, that your wholeness may be manifested in our lives.

> Revive your work, O God
> Exalt your precious name;
> And, by the Holy Ghost, our love
> For you and yours inflame. *(Written by Albert Midlane)*

Hear our prayer as we offer it in the name that is above every name. As we worship you this morning, may your love and joy flood our hearts. Give us a fresh vision of yourself. A fresh appreciation of your mercy and grace. This we ask through Jesus Christ our Lord. **AMEN.**

Scriptures for private prayer and reflection:

Lamentations 3:1-66 : 2 Timothy 4:1-8 : Revelation 14:1-13

Personal Prayer Topics:

_____

_____

_____

_____

_____

_____

43.

RACIOUS GOD, WE COME joyfully into your presence this morning. We thank you that you have made us part of your family. We are the recipients of your love and care. You have opened your heart to us and welcomed us into your presence. You have given to us a standing that we could never have had apart from your mercy and grace. So we worship and praise your name.

Forgive us, Father, when we have neglected to come to you when we have willfully disobeyed you; when we have not heeded the instruction of your Word. Forgive us, Lord, when we have hurt others and brought them disappointment, and sadness to you. Forgive us, Lord, when we have spoken hastily or struck out unthinkingly. Cleanse our thoughts and minds, from every stain of sin, through the sacrifice of Jesus on the cross.

Gracious God, meet with us this morning and change us. Renew our minds. Fill us with your Spirit. Equip us with your gifts. Some of us have had a hard week that has drained us of our strength and robbed us of our peace. Lord, we seek your grace to help us get our lives back into balance. As we worship you today, renew our strength. Enable us to take hold of the promises of your Word. Some of us are rejoicing in your goodness and in the opportunities you have given to us. Father, may our lives produce fruit that will last for eternity. This we ask in the name of Jesus. **AMEN**.

Let us have a time of silent prayer where we can bring to God the concerns we have for others:

Let us pray for . . . . (Expand these topics)

- Homeless people in our city as winter/summer approaches . . . .
- Families where one parent is in prison . . . .
- The work of Prison Fellowship . . . .
- The Salvation Army's social ministry . . . .
- Family life across our nation . . . .

Lord Jesus, so work in our lives, that we might be your faithful disciples. Release your Spirit into our hearts in a new way. May our lives overflow with generosity as we manage the resources that you have given to us. Grant us wisdom, and grant us courage, for the living of these days. May the image of Christ be more clearly seen in us as we go about our daily duties this coming week. We ask this through Jesus Christ our Lord and Master. **AMEN**.

Scriptures for private prayer and reflection:

Matthew 25:31-40 : John 11:17-44 : Romans 1:6-7

Personal Prayer Topics:

_____

_____

_____

_____

_____

_____

_____

_____

44.

ALMIGHTY GOD, IT IS with a great sense of anticipation that we gather for worship this morning. You have given us your Word that you are present with us. You have given us your Spirit, to transform our feeble thoughts and words into majestic praise and worship. We come before you with a deep longing to reach out and touch you and to receive from you that which we need.

So often unreality permeates our souls, and unbelief cripples our minds and sin paralyzes our spirits. Break through these barriers. We pray O Lord that we may hear your voice and see your glory and rejoice in your powerful activity.

Gracious God, you have extended to us your forgiveness. You have empowered us by your Spirit. Day by day you instruct us from your Word. For these and all your many mercies, we praise and magnify your holy name. So our Father, direct our worship we pray. Lead us into that place where our lives can be changed, our relationships enhanced, and our work can be transformed into service for you and bring glory to your holy name.

Let us have a time of silent prayer and reflection:

Heavenly Father it is in moments like this that we realize afresh how wonderful you are. We thank you that there is never a moment when we need to be out of touch with you. Accept our thanks in Jesus' name. **AMEN**

Let us pray for . . . . (Expand these topics)

- Family life across our nation . . . .
- The many "street kids" in our cities . . . .
- The Church around the world . . .
- A clear presentation of the Good News in churches . . . .

Gracious God, you have called us into a community where together we are dependent on your strength and power; where we need the leading of your Spirit every moment to guide us; where we need the encouragement of one another to persevere. Build us into a redemptive community we pray, where broken lives can be made whole; where hurting lives can be healed; where despair can be turned into hope. Lord God, you have made us workers together with you, that the lost may be found; that the wanderers may be brought home. Minister to us today to this end, through Jesus Christ our Lord. **AMEN**.

Scriptures for private prayer and reflection:

Psalm 26:1-12 : John 17: 6-19 : 2 Corinthians 6:14-18

Personal Prayer Topics:

_____

_____

_____

_____

_____

_____

_____

_____

45.

O LORD OUR GOD, THESE are demanding days in which we are living. So many pressures zero in on us. We just thank you this morning that we can pause in the midst of it all and fellowship with you and experience your renewing grace. We thank you for the provision of this day that we might spend time with you; that we might block out the many voices that clamour for our attention, and listen to you.

You have called us in Christ to be your people. You have given to us the gift of your Holy Spirit. You have led us to worship you in spirit and in truth. So this morning, we join our voices together in praise and magnify your holy name.

Yet, O Lord, we are very conscious of the fact that our lives don't always reflect the Christ likeness that you desire. Anxiety disturbs our peace. Fears rob us of our confidence. Personality clashes damage our love. Forgive us we pray. Strengthen us where we are weak. Affirm us where we are strong. May your Spirit continue His refining work in our souls that we may more faithfully walk in the steps of the Master. **AMEN**

Let us have a time for silent prayer and reflection:

Let us pray for . . . . (Expand these topics)

- Those who are seeking new jobs and presently unemployed . . . .
- Those who are facing financial difficulties . . . .
- The Church to have courage to witness in the power of the Spirit . . .
- Those whose lives have been damaged by the sins of others . . . .

Lord Jesus, as we focus on your Word today, give us eyes that recognize your truth. Enable us by your Spirit to interpret it into our daily lives and thereby bring glory and honour to your holy name. This we ask through Jesus Christ our Lord and King. **AMEN.**

Scriptures for private prayer and reflection:

Psalm 25:1-22 : Joshua 1:1-18 : Proverbs 29:18-27

Personal Prayer Topics:

_____

_____

_____

_____

_____

_____

46.

GOD OUR FATHER, WE come into your presence with thanks upon our lips. You have been so good to us. You have prospered us in so many different ways. You have opened your heart to us and we have seen the depth and reality of your love for us. Through your Son the Lord Jesus Christ you have extended to us your forgiveness and made us members of your family. There are times, O Lord, when we find this very difficult to understand, but we thank you that it is a reality and that we can call you "Father". As we look around us today our world is struggling from one crisis to another, aimlessly seeking its own solutions. Lord, have mercy on our world, and give direction to those who have the responsibility of leadership. We bless you, O Lord, that you are Sovereign in all the affairs of this world. You hold the whole world in your hands. We confess, that at times, we find this hard to believe - for so often it seems as though evil has the upper hand, but that is why we need the encouragement of your Word and the company of your presence.

Thank you, Father, for ministering to us by your Holy Spirit. Giving us new life; imparting to us your gifts for ministry; sanctifying us for your service. We thank you this morning for the victory that we have in Jesus Christ. Victory over the powers of darkness; victory over indwelling sin; victory over the power of our sinful human nature. We thank you this morning for the hope that you have given to us in your Son; that there is always a tomorrow with you. Focus our eyes upon the goal of our salvation this morning and grant us the grace to press on towards that goal with sensitivity and determination.

Father, we know that we fall far short of all that you have set before us. We are so blind. We are so self-willed. Please forgive us. So often, O Lord, we rely on our own understanding rather than trusting ourselves to you with all our heart. Lord God, our failures weigh heavily upon our hearts as we come before you. You know what those things are, so we don't need to pretend as we bow in your presence. We live in a fractured world that every day leaves its mark upon our lives. Forgive us and restore us we pray to that close fellowship with you. Revive our flagging spirits. Restore to us the joy of your salvation and reinstate us in the centre of your will and purpose for our lives. We thank you that this is possible through our Lord Jesus Christ – who died that we might be forgiven and who died to make us good, that we might go to heaven when our service is complete, saved by His precious blood. **AMEN**

Let us have a time for silent prayer and reflection:

Father, we bring the needs of the world around us to you. We pray for . . . . (Expand these topics)

- The industrial problems that plague our modern society and cause suffering to so many . . . .
- Those seeking employment that they may find it . . . .
- Those people whom we dislike for one reason or another . . . .
- The summer camps / winter retreats that are underway that many will find Christ . . . .

- Our city that the direction of its life may be changed and that the powers of darkness may be cast down. Give a new spiritual direction to our city we pray . . . .

Father, as we turn to your Word, open our eyes, we pray, to see what you are saying to us. Make us sensitive to the working of your Holy Spirit. May we be responsive to you. Father, minister to us, in order that we may minister to others. So grant us your grace this morning to become the people that you want us to be. This we ask through Jesus Christ our Lord and Saviour. **AMEN**

Scriptures for private prayer and reflection:

Matthew 10:19-20 : John 3:1-21 : John 14:15-31 : Romans 8

Personal Prayer Topics:

_____

_____

_____

_____

_____

_____

_____

47.

OUR FATHER AND OUR God, we praise and worship you this morning. You have done so much for us and we are so grateful. Your grace has been extended to us in boundless measure. Your strength has upheld us in stressful circumstances. Your love has encompassed us and made us know that we are part of your family. Your presence has dispelled our loneliness. Your peace has provided the calm we needed in the storms that have raged around us and within us. We bow before you with thanksgiving not only in our hearts but also on our lips.

As we worship today may our hearts and minds be completely open to you. May our eyes focus on those things that are eternal. May we learn afresh to surrender ourselves to your gracious keeping. It is in moments like these that we see our sinfulness and our unworthiness. We ask forgiveness, Lord, when we treat worship lightly; when it becomes an extra in our lives rather than our central focus. Lord, forgive us, when we go about our daily routines and virtually ignore you; when we fail to look for the places where you are working; when we fail to seize the opportunities that you give to us to demonstrate your love and share the Good News. Thank you for Christ our Lord who is the Lamb of God, who takes away our sin.

So, Lord, draw us closer to yourself. Help us to get a fresh perspective on life. We pray that you will prune our lives, that we might become more fruitful. Spirit of God, descend upon us we pray, search our hearts, empower our wills, and sanctify our lives. These things we ask in the name of Jesus Christ our Lord. **AMEN**.

Let us have a time of silent prayer and reflection. Then let us repeat together the prayer that Jesus taught us . . . .

Our Father, who art in heaven, hallowed be Thy name.
Thy Kingdom come, Thy will be done, on earth
as it is in heaven.
Give us this day our daily bread; and forgive us our debts,
as we forgive our debtors. Lead us not into temptation,
but deliver us from evil. For Thine is the Kingdom,
the power and the glory, forever. **AMEN** (Matthew 6:9-13)

Let us pray for . . . . (Expand these topics)

- The spiritual renewal of our country . . . .
- India where there is mounting persecution of the Church . . . .
- Those working for peace between the nations of the world . . . .
- Those who are nurses and doctors in our hospitals . . . .
- The threat of terrorism and those who are enacting it . . . .

So throughout this time of worship, we pray that you will renew us and refresh us. Speak to our hearts the Word that we need to hear and enable us by your Spirit to act upon it. This we ask through Jesus Christ our Lord. **AMEN**.

Scriptures for private prayer and reflection:

Romans 12 : Romans 13 : John 6:60-71 : Psalm 126:1-6
Ephesians 4:1-16

Personal Prayer Topics:

_____

_____

_____

_____

_____

_____

48.

RACIOUS GOD, WE DELIGHT to proclaim your name - to bow before you this morning in worship and to rejoice in your presence. We thank you that your love for us does not depend on our performance, but on your grace. Your faithfulness towards us is new every morning - Your strength is available to us every moment of every day. So we worship you today. You are our God and you have graciously made us your people.

O Lord, we are still in the process of growing as your people. We err in our judgements. We utter words that hurt and damage relationships. We seek things that are not on your list of priorities for us. Sometimes we shut our eyes to the opportunities that you set before us, so Lord, we pray that you will forgive us as we bow quietly in your holy presence.

Let us have a time for silent prayer and reflection:

So many countries are in chaos. People are seeking freedom and can't find it. Many are hungry and dying while others wastefully enjoy plenty. Others are persecuted by their governments. Lord God, have mercy on your world. May your Church rise to the occasion and demonstrate that true freedom can only be found in you, and that inner hunger can only be satisfied in Christ, who is the Bread of Life.

We desire this morning more than anything else, that you minister to each one of us. You know the deep needs of our hearts. You alone are able to free us from those things that hinder us from being like Jesus. Empower us we pray, that we might live for you in the power of the Holy Spirit. Mighty God, open our eyes to behold your glory.

As the hymn writer says, grant us courage, and grant us wisdom, for the living of these days. May Christ be seen more clearly in us as we go about our daily duties in this coming week. We ask this through Jesus Christ our Lord and Master. **AMEN.**

Scriptures for private prayer and reflection:

Proverbs 3:1-35 : Matthew 5:17-21 : Matthew 6:25-34
Romans 5:1-21

Personal Prayer Topics:

_____

_____

_____

_____

_____

_____

49.

William C. Dix focused our attention on Jesus when he wrote:

Alleluia! Sing to Jesus, His the sceptre, His the throne;
Alleluia! His the triumph, His the victory alone;
Jesus out of every nation has redeemed us by His Blood.

YOUR WORD, O LORD, encourages us to come into your presence singing with joy that you have placed within our hearts. We come before you with thanksgiving and praise, and lift up our voices in music and song. You are the King of Kings. You hold the whole world in your hands. Everything in it is yours. We bow before you in worship. We thank you for your gift of salvation and the privilege you have given us to declare this message and to declare your glory among the nations.

Let us have a time of silent prayer and reflection:

As we bow in your holy presence, we are not proud of the mistakes we have made. So often, our failures outnumber our successes and triumphs. Lord God, we seek your forgiveness for our stupidity and our obstinacy; for the sinful blindness of our hearts towards the opportunities you have given us. Forgive us, Father, for the wrong choices we have made, that have grieved you, and robbed you of your glory. Humbly and gratefully, we open our hearts to receive your miracle of grace. We thank you for the fresh, strong wind of your Spirit, who comes to bring us spiritual refreshment, cleansing and peace. Re-engage us we pray in your service.

We pray for your Church in countries where they persecute your people. Grant your grace to those who are in prison for Christ. Sustain those families who have lost loved ones. The Enemy is working hard to silence your Church. Enable your people to stand their ground and to live and proclaim your Word with boldness in the power of the Holy Spirit.

So Lord, as we meditate on your Word and lift our voices in praise, speak to our hearts, grant us courage to witness. Guide and empower us by your Spirit. We ask this through Jesus Christ our Lord and Saviour. **AMEN**

Scriptures for private prayer and reflection:

1 Thessalonians 3:6-13 : 1 Thessalonians 5:1-28 : 1 Peter 1:1-12

Personal Prayer Topics:

_____

_____

_____

_____

_____

50.

RACIOUS AND WONDERFUL LORD, we join our hearts and voices together this morning in praise and worship. How great you are! Creation is your handiwork. You hold the world in your hands. You are supreme in the universe. You are the unshakeable foundation of our lives in Jesus Christ. We thank you for your unfailing love towards us; for the gift of eternal life through our Lord Jesus Christ. Day by day you watch over us and provide for us. We thank you for the gift of family and friends who enrich and share our lives. We thank you that in Jesus, your love is fully expressed. We thank you that He was known as the "Friend of sinners", and that He shared His plans and His work with ordinary people like us. We thank you Lord, that you call us your friends.

Let us have a time for silent prayer and reflection:

We acknowledge before you that this friendship has not always seemed real to us. We are sorry that so often we are anxious as if you were not there. We are sorry that we do so little to make your friendship real to other people who do not know you. We recognize, O Lord, that so often it is our personal sins that put a barrier between you and us. You have told us in your Word that we should be holy in all that we say and do. So today we come and ask for your forgiveness and that you will show us how to become better friends and followers of Jesus.

So in this hour of worship minister to us to that end we pray. Reveal your will to us and grant us the grace to obey. This we ask through Jesus Christ our Lord and Saviour. **AMEN**

Let us pray for . . . . (Expand these topics)

- Local and national government . . . .
- Spiritual renewal in the Church . . . .
- Countries where there is terrorism and outright war . . . .
- Those who are friendless in our society . . . .
- Those who work in the educational system (Teachers, Administrators)

Thank you Lord for hearing our prayer. In Jesus name we pray. **AMEN**

Scriptures for private prayer and reflection:

Genesis 1:1-2:2 : Psalm 19 : Ephesians 2:1-10 : Romans 1:18-32
Romans 8:18-28

Personal Prayer Topics:

_____

_____

_____

_____

_____

_____

_____

51.

ALMIGHTY GOD AND GRACIOUS Heavenly Father, there is no one like you in the entire world. You shower your blessings on the just and the unjust. You love us even when we turn our backs on you. Lord God, as we come into your presence this morning, we recognise that you are holy. We read in your Word, "My thoughts are not your thoughts, neither are your ways my ways, declares the Lord. As the heavens are higher than the earth, so are my ways higher than your ways and my thoughts than your thoughts". You know every detail of our lives. You know where we have been and where we are going. We cannot hide anything from you. So you graciously reach out to us in mercy and grace, to forgive us, to clean up our lives and to enable us to be more like Jesus. How we marvel at the mystery of your love.

Lord God, you have invited us to ask, to seek, and to knock, assuring us in your Word, that if we ask, it will be given to us; if we seek, we will find; and if we knock a door will be opened to us. Help us to believe this, Lord. Enable us by your Spirit to live more by faith than by sight and to be more responsive to your Word. Take from us, we pray, that spiritual blindness that so often impedes us on our way.

Help us, O Lord, to live our lives in daring faith and humble trust. Draw us closer to yourself this morning. May your words speak to our hearts and direct our thoughts. Grant us your grace to respond to you. Lord, you have nudged us many times, but we have failed to respond to you. May today be different.

We pray that this morning we will open our lives to you in a new way and allow your Holy Spirit to perform that necessary spiritual surgery on us, so that we might know that it is well with our soul. This we ask through Jesus Christ our Lord. **AMEN**

Let us have a time of silent prayer to focus on the fact that Jesus is among us:

Mighty God, we thank you for your presence among us and for the wonderful way in which you have ministered to us. We worship and adore you. Change us we pray that we may be more like the Lord Jesus Christ, in whose name we pray. **AMEN.**

Scriptures for private prayer and reflection:

2 Chronicles 6:1-42 : Isaiah 55: 8-9 : Psalm 4:1-8
Matthew 6: 7-8 : John 17:1-26

Personal Prayer Topics:

_____

_____

_____

_____

_____

_____

52.

GOD OF GRACE AND God of glory, we bow in your presence Lord Jesus, with praise on our lips and thankfulness in our hearts. As the hymn writer puts it:

There was no other good enough to pay the price of sin
He only could unlock the gate of heaven and let us in.

(By Cecil Frances Alexander)

We thank you, Father, that you sent Jesus into the world to be our Saviour and Lord. We thank you for your forgiveness and the gift of eternal life. We thank you for the gift of your Holy Spirit, who dwells within us, granting us understanding of your Word and equipping and empowering us for your service in the world. As we worship you this morning, refresh us in mind and spirit, so that our lives may reflect your love and grace.

Lord, as we come before you today, some of us are distracted by the events that are taking place in our lives. Some of us are hurting and need your healing touch. Some of us maybe are wrestling with issues of faith. Lord Jesus, meet with us this morning, reveal yourself to us and enable us to receive from you that which we need. Our Father we pray, wash our souls with your redeeming grace so that we might be made whole.

Let us have a time for silent prayer and reflection:

So Lord, hear the prayers that we have voiced in our hearts to you this morning. We ask this in Jesus' name. **AMEN**

Let us pray for . . . . (Expand these topics)

- Those who are imprisoned in loneliness . . . .
- Those who are battling temptations . . . .
- Those who feel that life has cheated them . . . .
- Those whose work is monotonous . . . .
- Those who are seeking employment in a difficult market . . . .
- Those who are being persecuted because they are Christians

Mighty God, pour out your Spirit on us, open our eyes to behold your glory and to see the needs of the world around us as you see them, and equip us to serve you better. We ask this in the powerful name of Jesus. **AMEN**

Scriptures for private prayer and reflection:

John 4:27-42 : John 8:1-11 : Matthew 15:1-20
2 Corinthians 5:11-22

Personal Prayer Topics:

_____

_____

_____

_____

_____

_____

_____

Prayers for Special Occasions

1.

(CHURCH ANNIVERSARY)

OUR GRACIOUS GOD AND Father, as we come before you this morning, we acknowledge that you are greater in majesty than anyone can imagine. You are mightier in power than we are able to comprehend. You are more beautiful in holiness than we can perceive. You are much closer to us than we can ever realize. We just worship and adore you in humility and love.

We thank you for the founding members of this congregation and for their vision, their obedience and their enterprise. We thank you for their work of faith, their labour of love and their patient hope. We thank you for the fruit of their labours into which we have entered.

We ask your blessing in this day of opportunity. Lord, may our response to your calling be full, glad and free. Show us, we pray, where the real needs are. Strengthen our wills to do your work, and purify our hearts that we may see your face.

So bless this time of worship as we fellowship together with you. Leave the mark of your presence upon our lives, we pray, so that we may be recognized as your people. We ask this through Jesus Christ our Lord. **AMEN**

Scriptures for private prayer and reflection:

Psalm 84 : John 10:1-18 : 1 Corinthians 12 : 1 Peter 2:1-10

Personal Prayer Topics:

_____

_____

_____

_____

_____

_____

_____

2.

(MOTHERS' DAY)

EAVENLY FATHER, AS WE come before you this morning, we come with a deep sense of gratitude for all that you have given to us. We thank you for the resources that you have given to us, especially those significant people in our lives. We thank you this morning for the influence that our mothers and caregivers have had on our lives. At their knee we have learned love and trust. It was there that we so often learned to pray. Father, we thank you that they have freely given so much to us. This morning we would express our gratitude to you for them and the sacrifices they made that we might become what you planned we should be.

And Father, for all those other people who have touched our lives and influenced us and brought to us the love and grace of God, we thank you this morning. We thank you as well O Lord that so often you minister to us through the service of other people. Help us to ever be ready to receive what others may share with us.

Forgive us, Lord, if we have taken for granted all these good gifts to us. Forgive us, if we have done those things that have marred these precious relationships. Lord, this morning, touch our lives with your renewing grace. Fill our hearts with your love so that we might more clearly express your life within us.

Father, this morning, we pray for those whose families are fractured. Lord God, we ask that you will minister encouragement and strength to them and be to them all that they need.

We pray for our children that you will surround them with your great love, and influence their lives in such a way that they may come to know you early and become your disciples.

Lord God, we pray for those who are experiencing much inner pain because of broken relationships. You are the Great Physician and you can bring wholeness. So we ask that you will minister to each as they have need this morning. Father, we thank you that you are the comforter and sustainer of your people.

We pray for all O Lord, who seek to minister to the needs of families in our city. We think especially of . . . . (Name the person / organization) Give to them, we pray, much wisdom and compassion. Lead them by your Spirit to say and do those things that will encourage, strengthen and give hope to those who are despairing.

We bring before you the great issue of abortion that divides our society and robs the world of potential people. We pray that . . . . (Expand the prayer here).

Lord, our God, may your Word penetrate our hearts like a sharp sword – not to wound us but to heal us; not to hurt us but to restore us. Meet us in our hearts and minds this morning as we meditate on your truth. Let your joy be our strength today as we worship you. This we ask through Jesus Christ our Lord and King. **AMEN.**

Scriptures for private prayer and reflection:

Esther 1-5 : Romans 16:3-4

Personal Prayer Topics:

_____

_____

_____

_____

_____

_____

_____

_____

3.

(MOTHERS' DAY)

FATHER, THE WORLD AROUND us is celebrating Mothers' Day. We recognise, O Lord, that it has become just another commercial festival. But this morning we would seek to celebrate it in a spiritual way. Father, as we bow in your presence, we offer our thanks to you for setting us in families. We would thank you for mothers who took the time to show us love; who taught us how to pray; and who by their example conveyed to us the reality of the love of Christ. Maybe, for some today, our thinking about the family creates very negative thoughts. It brings back much pain and brings into focus a deep sense of loss. Lord God, enable us today to extend your forgiveness to any who may have hurt us - whether deliberately or unintentionally. May new channels of love and acceptance be opened in our lives.

Lord God, as we look around us today, we see so many things seeking to destroy the family and to make being a mother trivial and boring. Father, give us the grace and strength to oppose these trends, so the family can remain strong; so that the influence of Christian mothers may make its mark on their children and make it easier for them to love and serve you.

Father, there is so much brokenness in family life today. There is much pain and hurt. Lord God, pour out your Spirit on the family life of our nation. May each member of the family be enabled to begin anew to fulfil their God given responsibilities.

We pray for those who work with children that live in fractured families; with those who have been abandoned on the streets; that compassion and insight might be given to them so they help recreate those values and standards that are so necessary for positive living. May they be able to assist in the rebuilding of their damaged self-esteem. We pray for those mothers who have been physically and emotionally abused – sometimes even in the name of religion. Heal their pain we pray. Deliver them from their fears. Fill the emptiness that exists in their lives. Lord God, there is so much need in our world. Help us to do our part to alleviate some of the suffering we see around us. Help us to be sensitive and to demonstrate the love and forgiveness of Jesus.

Gracious God, we pray for homes this morning where mothers and fathers have failed, and where children have rebelled with drugs and promiscuity. Equip your Church, O Lord, to effectively minister in these areas, with understanding and integrity, so that lives can be changed by the power of the risen Christ.

In our home life, Lord, help us to model your truth and demonstrate your love, discipline, and grace. Make our homes places where others can find the Lord Jesus. May our homes be open to those around us who have needs. May we know that we serve your Kingdom as we minister in our homes. May our homes become an oasis to those who are struggling through the deserts of life. Father, when we fail you and one another, give us the grace to seek forgiveness and to acknowledge our shortcomings and get up and go on with the work you have given us.

So minister to us this morning, by your Holy Spirit, bringing us into greater conformity with your pattern for living. This we ask through Jesus Christ our Lord. **AMEN**

Scriptures for personal prayer and reflection:

Luke 1:26-38 : Luke 1:46-55

Personal Prayer Topics:

_____

_____

_____

_____

_____

_____

4.

(HARVEST THANKSGIVING)

OUR FATHER AND OUR God, we thank you for your promise that "while the earth remains, seedtime and harvest, summer and winter, day and night shall not cease". We thank you for the reliability of your Word and of the earth that you have made. You are the great Creator God and we worship you today. We praise you for the variety of the seasons and for the contrasts and the unity of your creation. We thank you that you have allowed us to enter into the earth's activity, that we can nourish the miracle of life and share in the bounty of harvest. How privileged we are that you have allowed us to work with you. O Lord, we are truly humbled, when we realise that we are dependent on a marvel that we have not manufactured. We just thank you this morning for all your blessings to us, and for providing us with everything that we need.

Lord, as we recognise the wonders of your world, we also see the ways in which man spoils it. Forgive us, Lord, for the way in which we exploit your world and squander its natural resources as though they belonged to us. Forgive us, that we are so wasteful, when others are without the basics of life. Lord God, as we look at the plenty and poverty in your world, may we not just see it as a problem of distribution, but as a spiritual problem that calls for changed lives and a recognition of Jesus Christ as Lord. Forgive us, Father, when the desire to get is stronger than the desire to give. Forgive us also when we are blind to the needs of others and to our own prosperity. Lord, change us we pray. Make us more responsible in the use of all your gifts. May we at all times recognise that you are the giver of all good and perfect gifts and that what we have is only on loan from you. Hear our prayer in Jesus' name. **AMEN**

Let us have a time of silent prayer and reflection:

Father, we come before you in intercession for . . . . (Expand the topics)

- Christian relief agencies – that they might have resources and personnel to help
- Those who find themselves in refugee camps around the world – for the sense of hopelessness that often pervades – for the medical needs – for the spiritual darkness
- The Third World and its special needs
- The Church in its caring ministry and proclamation of the Gospel
- Those suffering in any natural disaster . . . . (Name it and pray over the details)

Lord, as we are surrounded by the beauty of harvest may we not be blinded to the needs of those who have nothing or very little. As we see the great variety of gifts may we not be unmindful of those who experience scarcity. May the harvest not cause us to be sentimental but deepen our commitment to you and to one another. Make us wise stewards of your resources we pray. We ask these things in the name of Jesus Christ our Lord and Creator. **AMEN.**

Scriptures for private prayer and reflection:

Psalm 34 : Psalm 147 : Psalm 100 : Psalm 103

Personal Prayer Topics:

_____

_____

_____

_____

_____

_____

_____

_____

5.

(HARVEST THANKSGIVING)

*T*HIS MORNING WE ARE surrounded by such a wonderful display of different kinds of produce which is but a visual aid that reminds us of your goodness and faithfulness. Thank you so much for the joy we receive through such provision. We thank you for the ability to be able to appreciate all that you have given to us. Father, we think of those children who have never picked a flower and for those who have never climbed a tree because they live in concrete jungles or in areas that have been devastated by war. To them harvest is a very remote idea and 'thanks' seems very inappropriate. Lord, we bring before you today all who are deprived in this way.

Gracious God, the gifts that are displayed before us today are just part of our plenty. But there are millions who never have enough to eat - not only in distant places but also in our own city. Father, forgive us for our indifference to the needs of others. It is so easy for us, O God, to be forgetful of the fact that much of the wealth of our own country was gained by exploiting others. Grant O Lord that as a nation and as individuals, we may take seriously our responsibilities for those who are in desperate need.

Today, O Lord, we recognise your provision for our physical needs. But we would also remember that you are the provider of our spiritual needs as well. There are many millions today who do not know of your love for them and have never had the opportunity of responding to the claims of the Lord Jesus Christ. Father, make us eager and ready to share our faith in the same measure that we share our possessions.

Let's have a time of silent prayer and reflection:

Lord we come before you and pray for . . . . (Expand these topics)

- Those involved in agricultural research that will aid developing countries . . .
- Missionaries that are involved in teaching agriculture . . . .
- Those who receive practical help and encouragement from this church . . . .
- A harvest of righteousness in those who lead and sway public opinion . . . .
- Relief organizations . . . .

Father, make us more aware of others so that we might serve one another in the love of God and in the power of the Holy Spirit. Lord, enable us to walk more closely with you. May we ever seek to be ministers of reconciliation wherever we go - ministering the life of Christ and the grace of God. This we ask through Jesus Christ our Lord. **AMEN.**

Scriptures for personal prayer and reflection:

Psalm 92:1-15 : Psalm 113

Personal Prayer Topics:

_____

_____

_____

_____

_____

_____

_____

6.

(THE NATION)

OUR GRACIOUS GOD, WE thank you for our nation. For the freedom we enjoy. For the many material blessings that have come to us. You have been so generous towards us as a people. People from all over the world make up our country and we thank you for the rich diversity that you have brought together. We praise you that you are the sovereign Lord of history. The whole world is in your hands and that gives us renewed confidence this morning; otherwise the thought that events are the result of fate or chance would be very disturbing. You are establishing your Kingdom here on earth and you fashion history according to your divine plans.

As we pray for our nation, we know it is your will that people should worship you in the fellowship of your Church and then serve you in the life of the world. Send down upon our nation, O Lord, a spirit of repentance for the sinfulness which passes for broad-mindedness; for the apathy which calls itself tolerance; for the materialism which glories in its prosperity and then grasps for more. Have mercy on us, O Lord. Heal our land. Father, may faith and obedience walk hand in hand with this inward sorrow so that lives may be transformed; that integrity and godliness may characterise the people of our nation.

Sovereign Lord, you are the source of all goodness. We pray for those who are in positions of power and influence in our country. Give them, O Lord, the patience and courage to bear the burdens of state laid on them. May they know that they hold office because of your sovereignty. Enrich them, Father, with your grace and guide them by your Spirit that we may be governed with wisdom and godliness. We pray, O Lord, that you will watch over those who have the responsibility of helping to form public opinion - the press, the broadcasting services of radio and TV - the film makers - the internet gurus, that we may be enabled to exercise our rights as citizens in a manner which is responsible and in accordance with your will.

Father, we pray for your Church. Enable us to be the people you want us to be. Help us to be responsible citizens even though our primary loyalty is to your Kingdom. May we live as a redeemed people, manifesting that redemption in the care and concern that we show to your hurting and lost world. May we be a holy people - declaring that you have set us apart for yourself. May we be a united people in mind and spirit, so that your will can be accomplished. May we be a missionary people - seeking to reach others with the good news of salvation in Christ and that new beginnings are possible with Him. May we be a people who are gladly submissive to the truth of your Word as we see it in the Lord Jesus Christ.

Heavenly Father, help us not to lose our sense of spiritual balance as we work through the different agencies of our world. May we not lose sight of why we are here and what we should be doing. Keep us, we pray, from being negatively critical. Grant that we may be your ambassadors. Continually put your pressure on us to

CONVERSATIONS WITH GOD

pray for our land that it may prosper and that out of its prosperity
it may be able to assist those less fortunate. Lord God, hear the
concerns of our hearts this morning as we pray for our country
and as we offer ourselves afresh to you in the name of Jesus Christ,
the King of Kings. **AMEN**

Scriptures for personal prayer and reflection:

Isaiah 2:1-5 : Psalm 46 : Romans 13 : 1 Peter 2:13-25

Personal Prayer Topics:

_____

_____

_____

_____

_____

_____

_____

7.

(THE FAMILY)

O LORD OUR GOD, WE praise you that you have chosen to enrich our lives by your presence and by the generosity of your gifts to us. We thank you that you have set us in families. We bless you for the joys of family life, and thank you for all that we have learned about relationships, love and responsibility. In your great wisdom, O Lord, you meant the family to be a replica of the relationships that exist between the Father, Son and Holy Spirit. Lord, you have set before us a model on which to pattern our family life. When Jesus came it was within the context of a family.

It is comparatively easy for us to thank you for the joys and privileges of family life. But we recognise that sin has marred all our relationships and made them less than what you planned they should be. We do thank you even for those tense and strained moments, for so often these have been growing points that have led on to greater maturity under the direction of your Spirit. We think, O Lord, of those sleepless nights with children and elderly relatives that have taught us patience and compassion. We thank you that you work all things together, good and bad, for the benefit of the people that love you.

Let's have a time of silent prayer:

As we come before you this morning, we ask your forgiveness for those things that have spoiled our family life. Forgive us Father that sometimes we fail to show respect and understanding and love for one another. When we have hurt one another, please forgive us. Sometimes, O Lord, we neglect each other, by failing to pray for one another. O God, it is frighteningly easy to spoil that good relationship that you have planned for us by our selfishness and thoughtlessness. Forgive us, Lord, we pray.

Our Father, we think of that greater family, your Church. We pray that we may bring into it those things that will honour you and bless others. May we ever seek to preserve the unity of your family. May we never be found guilty of those sins that divide your Church. So Lord, cleanse us from our sins we pray. Heal those memories that cause us pain and hurt and restore to us the joy of our salvation, and positive relationships through Jesus Christ our Lord. **AMEN**.

We pray today for . . . . (Expand these topics)

- Those who are anticipating marriage in the near future . . . .
- Those whose marriages are under great stress . . . .
- Those whose homes have been broken up by divorce and separation . . . .
- Those who are single and those who have lost loved ones . . . .
- All the children in our families . . . .
- Elderly relatives in the eventide of life . . . .
- Those of our families who are separated from us by the miles . . . .
- Those whose family life has been disrupted by war or civil strife . . . .

Gracious God, we thank you that you are on the throne and that as we submit ourselves to you, so you will order our steps. Lord, may we pattern our life together on what you have revealed to us in your Word. This we ask through Jesus Christ our Lord. **AMEN**

Scriptures for private prayer and reflection:

Deuteronomy 6:1-25 : Matthew 12:46-50 : 1 Timothy 3:1-16
Acts 16:1-5

Personal Prayer Topics:

_____

_____

_____

_____

_____

_____

_____

8.

(FATHERS' DAY)

RACIOUS GOD, WE BOW in your presence this morning thankful that you are our Father, and that you are the hope and foundation of our lives. As we look around us we see so much that creates despair within our hearts. We thank you this morning for your love and grace and for your power to bring change and new direction to each and every one of us. As we read our daily newspapers we see that multitudes of people are confused and confounded. They don't know which way to turn. They have lost all sense of direction and purpose. Lord, we pray, pour out your Spirit upon us so that we may receive new vision and direction. Lord God, in this disjointed world, make us strong. Revive our hearts so that we may worship you in spirit and in truth. Father, we ask that you will channel your power through our lives so that change may come to others and we ourselves might also be transformed.

Lord God, we confess before you this morning that we have become complacent. We have sought our own will more often than yours. We confess O Lord, that we have been so easily diverted from walking in your ways. We recognise, O Lord, that so often we interpret your Word selfishly, because it suits our purposes. Father, forgive us and cleanse us from all our sin. Renew a right spirit within us.

Across our nation today, people are celebrating Father's Day. For some this is very difficult because there is no father in the home. For others it is difficult because the example that has been set is very negative. Lord God, this morning we pray for every father, and for those about to be fathers, that you would pour out your Spirit upon them. Grant to them, we pray, a sensitivity of spirit, a caring heart and a desire to do your will. Gracious God, you intended that fatherhood should be patterned on you. What we see in you and your activity among us your children, you desire that we should duplicate in our own family life. Help us, Lord, so to live. We pray this morning for those who abused their privilege of fatherhood and have caused hurt and pain in the lives of others, and have distorted their children's ideas about you. Forgive all such we pray, and minister to them by your Spirit through your Word. Lord God, we pray that you will raise up men who set a Godly example, who realise their own frailty, and who know what it means to sacrifice. Gracious Lord, where there has been hurt, bring healing. Where there is emptiness, fill it with your wonderful presence. Where there is anger and bitterness bring forgiveness and understanding. Lord God, we pray, renew the family life of our nation. We ask this through Jesus Christ our Lord. **AMEN**

Let us have a time for silent prayer and reflection:

Lord God we pray for those who . . . . (Expand these topics)

- Are involved in the ministry of counselling both at a Christian and secular level
- Are struggling with habits that are destructive of family life, that you will give them victory over the forces within them

- Are involved in the ministry of "Focus on the Family". We pray for their radio ministry and the many publications that are produced, that you will use these to enrich family life across the continent
- Are children who have been damaged by parental abuse. Bring healing and wholeness to their distorted world
- Are involved in social work, that they will ever remain sensitive to real needs and be enabled to help those who need guidance and support

Father, we live in a needy world. Only you can meet those deepest needs of the human heart. Enable us to be your ministers among the people that we know. May your Word guide us and feed us; may your Spirit equip and empower us for the tasks ahead of us; may our worship today bring us into a closer walk with you. So Father, as we meditate on your Word this morning, enable us to listen carefully, to obey willingly, and to serve you faithfully. This we ask through Jesus Christ our Lord and Saviour. **AMEN**

Scriptures for private prayer and reflection:

Ephesians 6:1-9 : 1 John 4:7-21

Personal Prayer Topics:

_____

_____

_____

_____

_____

_____

_____

_____

9.

(EASTER SUNDAY)

The Scripture says: "The stone that the builders rejected has
become the head of the corner. This is
the Lord's doing; and it is marvellous in
our eyes. (Mark 12:11)
This is the day that the Lord has made; let
us rejoice and be glad in it".
(Psalm 118:24)

GRACIOUS GOD, WE THANK you for all your goodness
to us, and especially at this time of Easter as we rejoice
in the knowledge of Christ's victory over death and the
grave. Help us to understand and appreciate more deeply all that
the resurrection means and may we show in our lives that joy
which belief in Christ's promise brings, and so draw others into
the experience of your love and its power to change lives and
make us citizens of your Kingdom.

O God our Father, forgive us for the poverty of our worship, our
neglect of fellowship and our hesitating witness to Christ. Forgive
us for any evasion of our responsibilities in your service, and our
imperfect stewardship of your gifts. Forgive us, Lord, when we

have been thoughtless in judgement, hasty in condemnation and grudging in forgiveness. Touch our lives with your renewing grace, we pray. Minister to each of us this morning, so that we may be true ambassadors of our living Lord and Master Jesus Christ, in whose name we pray. **AMEN**

Let us meditate silently - on these words of Scripture:

"But if it is preached that Christ has been raised from the dead, how can some of you say that there is no resurrection of the dead? If there is no resurrection of the dead, then not even Christ has been raised. And if Christ has not been raised, our preaching is useless and so is your faith." (1 Corinthians 15:12-14)

O Lord God, you are the bridge over troubled waters. You can lift us out of despair. You can remove our sense of hopelessness. You can replace our uncertainty with confidence. You can do this because you overcame sin and death and brought immortality to light. Mighty God, we pray that this will comfort those who mourn and those who sense their loss of loved ones; that you will comfort them as they seek to rebuild their lives. We pray for the children who have lost parents and who find themselves in a fog of confusion, battling with conflicting emotions. Minister to them, we pray, through counsellors and family members. We pray that you will pour out your Spirit on your Church that it may be able to express your compassion and be able to minister to the various needs of the hurting world around us. So may this time of worship prepare us more adequately for the service you want us to give. This we ask through Jesus Christ our risen Lord and Saviour. **AMEN**

Scriptures for private prayer and reflection:

Ephesians 1:1-15 : 1 Peter 1:3-9
1 Corinthians 15:1-8, 12-28, 54-57

Personal Prayer Topics:

_____

_____

_____

_____

_____

_____

_____

10.

(PENTECOST SUNDAY)

OUR FATHER, WE SAY with the Psalmist this morning, "Bless the Lord, O my soul, and all that is within me bless His holy name". For indeed Lord, you have done great things for us, and we are glad and rejoice in your goodness. On this Pentecost Sunday, we thank you for the gift of your Holy Spirit, who dwells within us; who guides us each step along the road of life; who assists us when we pray. We thank you that you have made our bodies temples of your Holy Spirit. With the hymn writer we ask:

> Breathe on me Breath of God
> Till I am wholly Thine,
> Until this earthly part of me
> Glows with Thy fire Divine. *(By Edwin Hatch)*

Gracious God and Father, we have come here with only one purpose this morning and that is to meet with you - to listen to what you have to say to us and to positively respond in worship and service.

We acknowledge that our lives are far from what you want them to be. Forgive us, we pray, for those things that keep us from doing your will. You have called us to love you with all our being and our neighbour as ourselves. Yet we must confess that our love at times has been half-hearted and at times we have been indifferent to our neighbour. Forgive us we pray. Remove the barriers that would keep us from hearing what you want to say to us this morning.

Let's have a time of silent prayer and reflection:

Father we pray for . . . . (Expand these topics)

- The leaders of our nation . . . .
- Those in military service in _____ (Name countries) . . . .
- The outpouring of the Holy Spirit on your Church . . . .
- This community in which we live . . . .
- The missionaries we support . . . .
- Those imprisoned and persecuted for their faith . . . .

So, our Father, hear the prayer of our hearts this morning. Speak to us at our point of need and by your Spirit enable us to respond to your love and grace. We ask this in the name of Jesus Christ our Lord. **AMEN**

OFFERING PRAYER:

Lord God, as we prepare to worship you with the presentation of our offerings, we ask that we may give with the spirit of joy in our hearts; that our giving may be indicative of our sacrifice and that our giving may glorify your name through Christ our Lord. **AMEN.**

Scriptures for private prayer and reflection:

John 14:15-27 : Acts 2:14-21 : Romans 8 : 1 Corinthians 3:16

Personal Prayer Topics:

_____

_____

_____

_____

_____

_____

_____

_____

11.

(YOUTH SUNDAY)

*W*E CELEBRATE TODAY WHAT you are doing in our Sunday School and youth organizations. (*List groups specific to your church.*) We thank you for your ministry among our children and young people. We thank you for those who have committed their lives to you; for those who have heard your call to service; for those who have chosen careers that will equip them to be your ambassadors wherever they go.

We pray today for all those who work with young people - youth ministers, club leaders, social workers, and organizational leaders. We thank you for their dedication. We pray that you will give them the ability to convey to the young life of our nation, the reality of your presence and the dynamic nature of your power to change lives and circumstances. As young people learn the art of leadership, we pray that you will inspire them to be able to communicate with their peers and bring them to knowledge of yourself.

We pray for all church youth groups, as they plan . . . . *summer camps, overseas ministries etc* . . . that through these activities, many young people will come to know Christ as their Lord and Saviour.

So Lord, hear the cry of our hearts for the children and grandchildren in our families, that you will touch their lives with your redeeming grace. This we ask in Jesus' name. **AMEN**

Let us have a time of silent prayer – as we pray for those young people in our families. Let us remember them by name before the Lord. Let us pray that the Christ-like example of our lives may have a lasting effect on our children.

Lord God, we pray for all those who are parents. When we enter into this responsibility we are all learners. We pray that you will give to our young parents, wisdom and understanding; that you will fill their hearts with your love and discipline. For those of us who are grandparents we pray that you will give us the grace to be supportive without being intrusive, to be helpful rather than hurtful. Help us, O Lord, to train our children in ways that will prepare them for a productive future. May we be able to set before them an example that will encourage them to follow the Lord Jesus Christ and give their lives to Him.

Father, there are many forces along the road of life that would seek to destroy our children. There's the availability of drugs; the challenge of sexual encounters; the force of peer pressure; the seduction of certain kinds of music. We pray, O God, that you will protect them from those who would seek to ruin them. Enable our young people to have the courage to say "no" when temptation comes. Give them the grace to witness to their faith in you. Enable them to excel in leadership. So we pray that your rich blessing will rest upon every young person within our family circle and beyond. This we ask through Christ our Lord. **AMEN**

Scriptures for private prayer and reflection:

Psalm 1 : Proverbs 3:1-18 : Isaiah 11:1-4 : 1 Corinthians 13
2 Timothy 2:1-13

Personal Prayer Topics:

_____

_____

_____

_____

_____

_____

_____

12.

(FIRST SUNDAY OF THE NEW YEAR)

*L*ORD GOD, ON THIS first Sunday of a New Year, we gather together in thankfulness for all that you have done, but we are also caught up in a spirit of expectation of what you are going to do. On the basis of your faithfulness, we anticipate you will lead us forward as the months unfold.

We ask that you will lead us further along the path of prayer. May we see you at work in new and exciting ways in our community. In our worship, may we sense your presence in powerful and creative ways. Inspire our faith to reach out to you. Lead us by your Spirit, so that we may fulfil our mission in this community and beyond, thereby extending your Kingdom.

Forgive us, Lord, for the opportunities we have missed or spoiled. Forgive us for the attitudes that we have displayed that have hindered your working in the lives of others. Build into us new desires and new visions for the future.

So, gracious God, open our eyes to see where you are working, so that we might cooperate with you. May we not see problems as setbacks but as springboards to greater spiritual heights. As we step into the unknown way ahead of us, may your Word be a lamp to our feet and a light to our path. This we ask in the name of Jesus our Lord and King. **AMEN**

Let's have a time of quietness to meditate and reflect on the faithfulness of God:

Let us pray for . . . . (Expand these topics)

- The Church throughout the world, that it may fully share in the mission Christ gave it of reconciling people to God.

- Those who suffer for their faith and convictions and are tempted to turn back because the way is hard. That they may know the strength of the Lord so that their loyal witness may draw others to Christ.

- Every nation in the world that they may seek the way that leads to peace and that everywhere human rights and freedom may be respected and that the world's resources may be ungrudgingly shared.

Each of us, O Lord, has a ministry in this world. You have poured your love into our hearts that it might flow out to others. You have called us to be witnesses to the truth and to be channels of your grace. Enable us by your Spirit to fulfil our calling. Write upon our hearts the message we need to hear and share. The disciples of old, when they were taken before the council, were recognized as those who had spent time with Jesus. From the time that we have spent with you today, may those who live and work around us take note that we too, have been with Jesus. This we ask for His name's sake. **AMEN**

Scriptures for private prayer and reflection:

Joshua 1:1-9 : Isaiah 40:21-31 : Isaiah 42:1-9 : Hebrews 13:1-9

Personal Prayer Topics:

_____

_____

_____

_____

_____

_____

_____

13.

(MEMORIAL DAY / REMEMBRANCE DAY)

LMIGHTY GOD OUR FATHER, we come before you today with a deep sense of gratitude in our hearts for the many blessings you have showered on us as a nation. We thank you that you have enabled us to help other nations move into freedom. We thank you that we have been able to take the Good News of Jesus Christ all over the world. Yet we are reminded today, that those blessings and opportunities come with a high price tag. Lives have been lost, families have been bereaved. Today, O Lord, as we remember these things, we pray for lasting peace to move across our world and for the hearts of men and women to be changed.

O Lord, as Francis of Assisi prayed, hundreds of years ago, we would pray for ourselves and for others . . . .

Lord, make me an instrument of your peace;
Where there is hatred, let me sow love;
Where there is injury, pardon;
Where there is doubt, faith;
Where there is despair, hope;
Where there is darkness, light;
and where there is sadness, joy.
Gracious Master, grant that we may not so much seek to be
consoled as to console,
to be understood, as to understand;
to be loved, as to love.
For it is in giving, that we receive.
It is in pardoning, that we are pardoned;
and it is in dying that we are born to eternal life.

As memories flash across our minds today may we be reminded
that everything that is good always involves sacrifice. This we ask
though Jesus Christ our Lord. **AMEN**

14.

(CHRISTMAS DAY)

A T THIS TIME OF Christmas as we celebrate Christ's coming into this world, we are filled with wonder and amazement. You came to be with us, yet you remain far greater than we can ever imagine. You are near to us, yet your holiness and wisdom sets you apart from us. We know that you are among us, yet we are unable to describe your glory.

The Scriptures remind us O Lord, that all heaven broke forth in celebration when Jesus came to earth. We would join our voices with that of the heavenly chorus and say - "Glory to God in the highest and on earth peace to men on whom His favour rests". We just praise and magnify your holy name.

Through Christ you have granted us forgiveness of sins. You have given us your Holy Spirit, to guide and empower us. You have opened our eyes to see the truth revealed in your written Word and in the Word who became flesh and dwelt among us. Your strength has upheld us in stressful circumstances. Your presence has dispelled our loneliness. Your peace has brought us into a new relationship with yourself and provided the calm we needed in the storms that have raged around us.

Forgive us, Lord, when we take these things for granted, and allow the world's materialism to blind us to the spiritual significance of this time. Forgive us too, that so often our thanksgiving is confined to words rather than being demonstrated in our living. Deliver us we pray, from the seducing influences of evil.

As we worship you at this Christmas time, may your love and joy flood our hearts. Grant us a new vision of yourself; a fresh appreciation of your mercy and grace. This we ask through Jesus Christ our Saviour and Lord. **AMEN**

Afterword

As you have come to the end of this book, you can do a number of things. You can close the book and put it on the bookshelf and do nothing more. Some may well do this! Another response is to go back over what you have read and note the sections that you might have marked for some reason. This response is by far the most profitable. This would be my suggestion to you. Ask yourself –

- What did I learn from this book?
- How did it enrich my life?
- What impact has it had on my prayer life?

The priority activity in the Early Church was prayer and the proclamation of the Good News. The results were measured not in "ones and twos", but in thousands. Luke shows us this in the Acts of the Apostles.

Armin Geswein wrote, "If God is going to do it, it has to be by prayer." I grew up attending a church which had a prayer meeting every Saturday evening for two hours. It covered a multitude of topics. The interesting fact is that the church grew in every way. People found Christ. Others were called to serve the Lord in numerous ways - and I was one of them. In addition something significant happened in every service. Remember this was in England!

If this book assists in opening the door for God to act in your life and the life of the church, it will have achieved its purpose.

Donald Grey Barnhouse said, "I am not so sure that I believe in "the power of prayer", but I do believe in the power of the Lord who answers prayer."

* * * * * * * * * * * * * * * * * * *